His
o
Bluegrass
in
New York
and
Northeastern Pennsylvania

by

Ken Oakley
and
Carol Ripic

Phyllis
Hope you
enjoy our
book!
Ken n' Carol

1999
K&C Publications
Deposit, NY

ISBN: 0-9661351-1-3

Published by K&C Publications
11 Third Street
Deposit, NY 13754

Printed by
Courier Printing Corporation
Deposit, NY

To the memory of Ray 'Whitey' Fritz,
the epitome of a bluegrasser.
He shared his knowledge,
his instruments and his friendship
with all who knew him.

Foreword

We are indebted to the many bluegrass enthusiasts who provided so much information for this book through interviews, returned questionnaires and phone calls. Their input, anecdotes, loaned photographs and shared stories are greatly appreciated. Although this group numbers over one hundred, we regret that more could not have been approached. So, we have written *a* history, not *the* history of bluegrass in this area.

Much of history depends on what those who went before us have left behind for us to examine. The same thing is evident with information relevant to the contents of this book. Some individuals like Marge Crawford, Ray Fritz, Ron Parsons and Earl Wakeman have passed away and are no longer here to answer questions or resolve arguments. We were fortunate to have already interviewed Rudy Perkins before he passed away. Some organizations, like the Southern Tier Bluegrass Association, have kept meticulous records and memorabilia-filled scrapbooks since their organization. For others, very little information is available.

Bill Knowlton provided a great deal of information not only about himself but also about the bluegrass music scene in New York and Northeastern Pennsylvania in general. In addition he recommended the book *Old Time Music Makers of New York State* by Simon Bronner. Much of the material in the first chapter is derived from this valuable and interesting source.

Special thanks go to the individuals in the bluegrass biographies chapter. While there may be many others equally significant who might have been included, we feel that these twenty-five profiles provide a balanced portrait of the emergence of bluegrass in this area of the states.

Finally, although every attempt was made to verify information, errors may have occurred. We apologize to anyone inadvertently left out of a group, band, etc. and for any errors in the spelling of names. We would appreciate having corrections brought to our attention.

Ken and Carol
May 1999

Interviews

Many thanks go to the people who were interviewed in the course of writing this book. Their contributions permitted the presentation of a much broader perspective because the group included band members, emcees, organization members, instrument salesmen, sound men, festival site owners, parking lot pickers, radio announcers, promoters and fans. Of course, many fit into several categories.

Andy Alexander
Phil Alexander
Bill Anderson (Corning)
Bill Anderson (Groton)
Jolene Anderson
Maggie Anderson
Dave Armitage
Evelyn Baker
Louie Banker
Junior Barber
Mike Barber
Nick Barr
Jim Baudendistle
Tom Benson
Ed Berbaum
Geraldine Berbaum
Joe Bonafanti
Charlie Brown
Charles Burke
David Carey
Bernie Carney
Marlene Carney
Pete Carr
Gene Clayton

Dave Cleveland
Hank Clothier
Irene Clothier
Ray Correll
Jim Cram
Richard Crowley
Joe Davoli, Jr.
Steve Davey
Dave Denny
Dick DeNeve
John Delaney
Ray Delaney
Larry Downey
Carl Eddy
Dewey Edwards
Bobbe Erdman
Steve Feinbloom
William Forrest
Kim Fox
Leroy Frisbee
Jane Fritz
Eric Gibson
Leigh Gibson
Smokey Greene

Harry Grant
Dave Hampton
Jim Hannigan
Gary Harper
James Hartman
PatriciaHartman
Carl Hedges
Elmer Hoover
Stan Ink
Steve Jacobi
Larry Kelly
Carl Kithcart
Bill Knowlton
Bill Laing
Gil Laing
Clint Lainhart
Ted Lambert III
Walt Laubach Jr.
Daryl Lesch
Doug Lesch
Mary Lockwood
Steve Lundberg
Roy Matthews
Dale Maxwell
Brian Miller
Lucy Norton
Aline Oliver
Lynn Oliver
Mark Orshaw
Chris Panfil
Mark Panfil
Pat Parsnow

Craig Parsons
Verna Parsons
Dana Paul
Herbert Peet
Ron Penska
Rudy Perkins
Jim Pritchard
Tom Richards
John Rossbach
Carol Rumpf
Philip Schiebel
Bob Schneider
Gil Siegers
Stan Steinkamp
Rick Schaeffer
Gary Stout
Carl Stump
Bill Szabo
Frank Thrall
Maude Thrall
Don Towers
Doug Trotter
Jack Tryon
Steve Tryon
Bill Veasey
Bucky Wayne Walters
Helen Weldon
Kevin Whalen
Jeff Wisor
Albert Worthen
Ted Wrench

Picture Credits

Evelyn Baker, 81
Tom Benson, 27
Ed and Geraldine Berbaum, 19
Charlie Brown, 79
Frank Crawford, 23, 53
Jane Fritz, 117
Carl Kithcart, 74
Bill Knowlton, 135
Bill Laing, 138
Elmer Hoover, 130, 132, 166
Mary Lockwood, 144
Ken Oakley, 4, 6, 65, 100, 114, 115,
    119, 128, 141, 159, 168, 173
John Rossbach, 149
Mary Helen Steele, 162
Bill Szabo, 153
Helen Weldon, 71

Table of Contents

Prologue

The impression of this, his first festival, would remain with him long after these three days were over. During the supper break he took out his old Kay guitar to play a song he'd heard on stage. "The Wreck of Old # 97" used the only three chords he knew, G, C and D. Now, he was just sitting, soaking up the music being played by the three musicians who had drifted over to his camper.

He was a little embarrassed when the fiddler asked him if he would chord the "Black Mountain Rag" with him and the other two pickers. Professing ignorance about the chord changes, the beginner was impressed when the fiddler patiently explained what the chords were and when to use them. He even loaned him a capo and gave him a two-minute lesson on how to use it. The beginner watched, surprised, as the fiddler retuned his strings from regular to A-tuning. "Sounds better," he explained.

The man with the Kay guitar could not get over how good the music sounded, even with his ragged strumming and tardy chord changes. And when he decided to stop so that he could record what they were doing, they showed no inclination to leave his campsite.

Before they finally did leave, the guitar player showed him how to bar the first two strings at the third fret to get what he called a "bluegrass G." After hearing that the newcomer was thinking about getting a 5-string, the banjo player took the time to show, in slow motion, the TIMT-MITM forward-backward roll on his Gibson. To help the novice remember, the banjo player picked up a discarded program from a nearby table and wrote down the eight-note tablature.

As the shadows of the trees began to lengthen toward the opposite side of the festival grounds, the new recruit placed the Kay in its case. He put a new tape in the recorder and wandered over to the adjacent campsite where three motor homes were parked in a U shape, their awnings covering most of the enclosed space. For the next two hours he was immersed in a kaleidoscope of blurred sounds and images. He was glad he'd brought the tape recorder because he wanted to listen later to the mandolin player's rendition of "Rawhide." He was interested and a bit surprised to find that the fiddle and the mandolin were tuned alike.

As the daylight faded, the bass player rested his instrument on its side before lighting the tinder under the heavier logs piled in the rusted tire rim. Then he disappeared into his camper to "get some supper." His departure was followed by a short discussion about who should take his place. One of the two banjo players finally put his instrument down and picked up the bass. After making a few quick tuning adjustments he joined the others in a spirited rendition of "John Hardy." It was then that the new guy realized that many of the musicians were comfortable playing more than one instrument. Maybe he could, too. He listened more carefully to the cadence of the bass. When he began to anticipate the walk from one chord to the next and the double slap, he hoped that someday he, too, would be able to put down his guitar and pick up the bass.

About the time they were ready to call it a day, a young woman carrying a guitar case approached. They were still inclined to quit when she produced what looked like a guitar, except that this guitar had a round metal plate in the center of the top. Even though they were packing up to go, the young lady sat down on a folding stool she had carried with her and began to play. Someone told him later that her guitar-like instrument was a Dobro. About halfway through "Carter's Blues," the guitar player joined in, then the fiddler, and finally, all but two of the original pickers were playing. And they continued to play for another two hours.

The thing that impressed the beginner the most was the way she played an upbeat tune called "Fireball." From that point he just left his recorder on and joined in, sitting just outside the players' circle although they invited him to move in closer. During a lull he realized that his back ached, his fingers were throbbing and his recorder had shut down. Although he felt wide awake he remembered his bluegrass friend's advice to get a little sleep each night or be wasted the next day.

As he lay on the bunk inside his camper he could still hear the thump, thump of the bass punctuated by the mandolin, fiddle or banjo leads. He also realized how much better the songs sounded with two voices instead of just one. He couldn't fall asleep right away. Words and phrases he'd heard while attending the stage show and the picking sessions kept chasing around in his mind.... D-tuners, mountain modal, crosspicking, RB 250, circle of fifths, tabs, G run, double shuffle, up the neck. He couldn't remember them all and he promised himself before he dropped off to sleep that he was going to learn as much as he could about bluegrass music.

Instruments

Fiddle

One of the first artisans to produce a violin like the ones we use today was Andrea Amati (1511–1579) of Cremona, Italy. There is some speculation that he may have even been its inventor. The violin was preceded by a similarly shaped *rebec*, the *llyra*, the *kit* (a small pocket-sized version) and the *viele*. Amati's work was continued by sons, Antonio (1550–1638) and Girolamo (1551–1635). Nicola Amati (1596–1684) the son of Girolamo, was the master craftsman under whom Antonio Stradavari and Andrea Guarneri (1626–1698) learned their trade.

The most famous of these artisans, Stradavari (1644-1737) left the master Amati in 1680 and went on to fashion over 1200 fine violins, some still in use and greatly prized today. The basic shape of the instrument and method of playing did not change for the next three hundred years. The early settlers of this country brought with them the violin and the ability to craft its likeness.

Guitar

The familiar six-string guitar was introduced into Europe by the Arabs around the 14th century. It was preceded by the cittern, a smaller and narrower version which had from 8 to 14 strings. Antonio de Torres Jurado (1817–1892), a Spanish guitar maker, was responsible for the design of the modern guitar. He improved the top soundboard and standardized the string length to approximately 26 inches. He also perfected the use of fan barring, or bracing, to reinforce the underside of the sound board. Unlike the old Amati, Guarneri and Stradivari violins, it is not these early guitars that are preferred for bluegrass music but rather the ones made in this country. While there are many good American guitar companies at present, perhaps the most appreciated guitars are made by one in particular, the C.F. Martin Company. Christian Frederick Martin set up shop in New York City in 1833, but soon moved to Nazareth, PA, where his heirs still run the business today. Again it should be noted that the guitar was first brought to this country by early settlers.

Banjo

The tenor or four-string banjo and the five-string have as their ancestor the banjar, brought to this country by African slaves. In this country, the banjo was used primarily as a rhythm or percussion instrument even after Joel Sweeney added the drone fifth string in 1831. When played in a group, the banjo was used as a back-up instrument. However, when played as a solo instrument it carried the melody, the performer sometimes using one, two or three fingers, or even a plectrum. The banjo enjoyed popularity until about 1930 when its use fell into a decline that lasted until about 1945, when Earl Scruggs gave the instrument new life with his three-finger style instrumentals and tasteful backup rhythms.

Mandolin

The history of the mandolin is similar to that of the violin. It was developed in Europe from the lute and at first had a rounded belly body. A bit later, the back became flatter and the top was carved, as was the top of the violin. Like the guitar, the mandolins favored by bluegrass pickers are those made in this country, particularly the F and A models produced by the Gibson Company. The instrument of choice is the Lloyd Loar Gibson F model which most players say has the crispest and most melodious sound.

Bass

The bass, a later addition to the bluegrass band, is simply a larger version of the violin and its origins are the same as that of the violin family. It should be noted that the bass was not used in the early hillbilly or country bands which usually consisted of a guitar, fiddle, banjo and mandolin.

Dobro

And so we come to the sixth and most recent addition to the bluegrass band, the Dobro. Like the Hawaiian lap and steel guitars, chords and melody notes on the Dobro are created by a bar held in the left hand. The Hawaiian, lap and steel were already in use as country instruments when the four Dopyera (later changed to Dopera) brothers came to this country from Czechoslovakia in 1908. In 1926, one of the brothers, John, designed a steel bodied guitar into which he installed three aluminum resonators. Subsequently he, his brothers and some other investors formed the National String Instrument Company. In 1928, John and the brothers left the other investors and founded their own company called the Dobro Corporation. It is interesting to note that the name Dobro is derived from Dopera Brothers. It also means "good" in the Czech language. The company produced a wooden bodied guitar with a single resonator along with resonated mandolins and violins. It was the Dobro guitar, however, which became their best seller. The prewar models are especially prized by bluegrassers today.

With the advent of WWII and the subsequent metal shortage, National went out of business. Shortly after that interest in the Dobro waned and the Dopera brothers also went out of business. It was then left to Shot Jackson, Pete Kirby (Bashful Brother Oswald) and Josh Graves to carry on with the resonated guitar. When Graves joined Flatt and Scruggs in 1955 his Dobro playing revived and stimulated interest in the Dobro which has continued in bluegrass circles to the present. In fact, there was so much interest that in the 1960s the original Dopera Brothers went back into the business of making Dobros and were subsequently bought out by the Gibson Company.

This is not to say that other instruments cannot be used in a bluegrass band. A jaws harp may be used in a bluegrass novelty act. The harmonica and five-string Dobro are regularly used in some bands. For many years Alan Shelton played the five-string Dobro in the Jim and Jesse McReynolds' bluegrass band. Deposit resident Leo Strong played the five-string Dobro in **Gulf Summit Express**. Several local bluegrass bands have included harmonica players. Bob Mehan played one for a Pennsylvania-based band and Joe Ganna most recently played one in the Binghamton-based **Stateline**. When **Sweet Things** performed their string quartet at Wrench Wranch in the spring of 1992, they used a viola and a cello in addition to the fiddle and stand-up bass.

Moreover, these six instruments did not all become part of the bluegrass band at the same time. Nor were the earlier hillbilly and country music groups using only these instruments. What was to eventually become today's bluegrass band went through several transitions where other instruments such as the accordion, clarinet, tenor banjo, piano, saxophone and drums were sometimes used.

Considerations such as size, cost and availability determined the immigrants' choice of instruments. Because of this, not all the traditional bluegrass instruments were brought by the early settlers to this country. Marveling at the apparently unending bounty of cheap land, these newcomers pushed the indigenous people further and further west until finally many Indians emigrated to Canada. By the time of the Civil War much of the land comprising New York and Northeastern Pennsylvania consisted of small towns and farmland. The farmers, shopkeepers and tradesmen who now lived here brought across the Atlantic from France, Spain, Germany, Italy, Ireland, Scotland, Wales, Great Britain and other European countries their traditional stringed music as well as the guitar, mandolin and fiddle.

However, it was the fiddle which is most evident in the rural music from the time of the Revolutionary War to the 1920s. Small, light, relatively easy to make and capable of conveying the mood of the tunes played, the fiddle was often the only instrument providing music at barn raisings, bees, social gatherings, dances and other celebrations.

In this rural setting the fiddler of the family would pass on to the next generation not only the fiddle but also the skills necessary to play it. This practice continued until about 1920 when family members began to take up other instruments which allowed them to form the hillbilly bands. These bands lasted until the 1950s when the next generation would become the forerunners of today's bluegrass groups.

For those who lived in the towns and cities in mid-19th century America, music consisted of the popular songs of the day, orchestra and band music, and opera. Fiddle, banjo and/or guitar music wasn't really considered music *per se*. It was hillbilly, mountain or country music. Only rural or country folk had the hoedowns, house dances and work bees. People who lived in the cities, in general, looked down their noses at that particular kind of entertainment.

While the city dwellers were minding their stores, working in the factories and attending musicales and operas for their evening enjoyment, the rural people were tending their farms. For any leisure time entertainment the farmers had to provide their own music and providing their own music meant using the most readily obtained instruments such as the fiddle and banjo, very often both home made.

At the beginning of the Civil War both Union and Confederate farm boys went off to war. Some of these young men took either a banjo or a fiddle with them. It is common to open a pictorial book of that war and see somewhere in it a group picture where a man is holding or playing one of these instruments.

In a recent best seller, *Cold Mountain* by Charles Frazier, there is early in the book a mention of the battle of Fredericksburg in 1862. "Late in the afternoon the Federal quit coming and the shooting tapered off...somewhere above them on the hill a fiddle struck up the sad chords of

Lorena. The wounded Federals moved and keened and hummed between gritted teeth on the frozen field and some called out the names of loved ones."(Fraizer, 8-9)

And in the book, *Ship of Gold in the Deep Blue Sea*, by Gary Kinder there is a passage about a time a few years earlier, September 1857, which tells about a ship carrying passengers and a shipment of gold from California to the East Coast via the Panama Canal. "That evening at sunset, the first and second class passengers took supper at the long tables and railroad benches in the dining salon. Afterward they retired topside again to stroll in the cool evening breezes and amuse themselves with impromptu skits or readings, or poems put to music and accompanied by a banjo, a guitar, or an old fiddle."(Kinder, 22)

A 1923 Hollywood movie, *The Covered Wagon*, depicted the taming of the Old West at about the time of the Civil War. While neither the film nor its stars are remembered today, one of the promotion stills shows a young lad sitting on a flatbed wagon playing a five string banjo, probably an open back.

One last note about the fiddle and the Civil War. When Ken Burns produced the eleven-hour Civil War epic shown on PBS in 1990, he wanted authentic background music for the still photos which made up much of the program. One of the songs he selected was a fiddle tune composed and performed by Jay Unger, a New York State contemporary. "Ashokan Farewell" was written by Jay at the conclusion of a fiddle and dance workshop held in Ashokan, NY in the summer of 1982. In fact, that tune became the theme song of the program. Many who viewed the presentation were convinced that the tune was an actual Civil War era song.

After the Civil War and up until the 1920s the music which was to be the predecessor of bluegrass was found in house gatherings, fiddle contests, local square dances, barn raisings or work bees. At any of these gatherings, there would be present a farmer or perhaps a local from a nearby town who could play the fiddle. There would be singing and dancing, both round and square. Perhaps the fiddle would be joined by a guitar or banjo, or both. If one were available there might be a piano or an accordion as well. In some areas these gatherings grew to include regular musicals, both at individual homes and in public places like the Grange Halls or local school buildings. When these gatherings grew to be more regular, the music was performed by organized bands.

But first came the fiddlers.

The Fiddlers

One of the earliest fiddlers in rural New York State was an African-American man named Alva Belcher, born in Delhi, NY in 1819. Alva played throughout the Catskills area where he lived, both as a single entertainer and with his band of white musicians. In addition to Alva's fiddle, the band included a tenor banjo, guitar, piano and sometimes an accordion. A measure of his success and respect as an entertainer is evidenced by the fact that a fiddle tune from Ireland originally called "Mason's Apron" was renamed "Belcher's Reel." Alva also ran a grocery store in Delhi until 1879 when he sold the establishment to devote more time to his music. He died in Kingston, NY January 6, 1900.

Although Boney Quillan was not a fiddler, he did play the banjo and was famous throughout Delaware County for making up songs on the spot about raftsmen and local happenings. He was born May 15, 1845, lived most of his life in Hancock, NY and died in the Bath Veteran's Hospital June 6, 1918. Boney had been a Union soldier, teamster, logger and handyman. But he is best re-membered as a song-writing banjo player who rafted logs from the Hancock and Callicoon area down the Delaware River to the Chesapeake Bay. He was also reputed to be a moderately heavy drinker and there are many stories about his antics involving alcohol and deviltry. On one occasion he was reprimanded by his employer for not fastening all the straps and buckles on the team of oxen he was driving.

He was told that if he didn't have all the straps fastened properly the following day, he would be let go. When the owner came to check on Boney the next morning, the oxen were properly fastened, with every strap and buckle in place...one ox facing north and the other facing south. Boney had tendered his resignation.

'Happy' Bill Daniels was born in rural Vestal, NY in 1853 and was playing his fiddle professionally by 1872. He later moved to Varna, near Cortland, where he shared his musical knowledge with any interested youngster. In particular he had great influence on John McDermott to be introduced later in this chapter. Bill was well known in Central New York. It was said that no dance was complete without his presence. He died November 26, 1923.

Charlie Freer of Neversink, NY was another of the old time fiddlers. Charlie was born in 1867 and learned to fiddle before he was ten years of age. By the time he was twelve he was playing second fiddle for his father. He remembered the square and round dance platforms built at Readburn, Peakville, Shandelee, Callicoon, Obernburg, Hortonville and Shohola Glen. These platforms were lighted at night by lanterns hung on posts. He also recalled winning a square dance calling contest at the amusement park in Shohola Glen. He said that the dance platform there was large enough for 800 dancers though he could remember playing for about only 80. Other fiddlers of his time were Charles Eastman of Lackawack, a Civil War veteran, Frank Moore and Dietrich Berthoff of Divine Corners and Obediah Kortright of Hurleyville.

Other fiddlers of the Delaware County area from the turn of the century included George Bowers, from Tennanah Lake who also played a cello with the end pin resting on the seat of a chair, Will Brock and Dan Nutting from Liberty, Arthur Corsair from Trout Creek, William Goerke from Read's Creek, Jesse Hornbeck from Gooville, Zebadee Kelly Jr., Lew Beach, and John Day Lennox from Elk Brook, Bruce Lindsley from White Sulphur Springs, Ralph Masten from Monticello, Lawrence McGrath and

Abner Seeley from Livingston Manor, George Palmatier from Burnwood, and Jake Brigham and 'Fiddler Jim' Wheeler, a river man who was said to take his fiddle with him when he went to market, both from Fish's Eddy.

John McDermott was born in McLean, NY on April 2, 1869 of Irish immigrant parents. He became well known for his singing and fiddle playing. He said many times that he'd been influenced by the playing and guidance of 'Happy' Bill Daniels. In fact, John McDermott is credited with a fiddle tune called "Happy Bill Daniels' Quadrille." John moved to Cortland in 1894 to work as a wire weaver at the Wickwire Company. John, a perennial winner at New York State fiddle contests, once issued a challenge to all comers for the fiddling championship of the United States. When the challenge was not answered he claimed the title of the World's Champion Fiddler. During his tenure he played over radio station WFBL out of Syracuse, NY. He also played in a band with Harry French, piano, Don Kane, banjo and Bert Boice, drummer. Two of John's contemporaries were fiddlers Harry Westphal and Lou Christman. John died in Cortland on June 23, 1957.

Fred Woodhull is as well-remembered for his band, **Woodhull's Old Tyme Masters**, as for his fiddling ability. Fred was born in 1874 in Penn Yan, NY. He moved to Elmira in 1895 where he met and married Elizabeth Blanch Schmidt. Together they performed at house parties and dances, Fred on the fiddle and Elizabeth on the guitar. They had three sons, John, born in 1898, Herbert in 1902 and Floyd in 1903. It was Floyd who followed his father's choice of instrument by taking up the fiddle. Around 1920 the **Woodhull's Old Tyme Masters** band was formed with Fred and his three sons as the nucleus, although there were a number of other players in the band throughout the years which followed. The band played all over the central and southern parts of New York State, going as far south as Central Pennsylvania and as far east as Long Island. They also played regularly in their own establishment, The Barn in Elmira, NY. In 1939 they were honored by being asked to play at the NYS World's Fair in New York City. They played over radio stations WESG and WELM out of Elmira and WHCU out of Ithaca. They also made several recordings with Victor in 1941. When Fred died in 1946 he was replaced in the band by a fiddler named Ransom Terwilliger from Binghamton, NY. Shortly thereafter the band broke up and the boys went their separate ways. Only Floyd carried on with his music, making two albums with Folkkraft and playing with the McNett family for the opening of Fraley's Park in Waverly in 1977. Turning 80 in 1983, he finally quit performing in public.

Willard Kouf was born in 1881 in Schuylerville, NY near the Vermont border . He moved to the Ithaca, NY area prior to WWI and accompanied by his wife Alice, began fiddling at house parties. In Ithaca he and Alice raised four sons, Milo who took up the fiddle like his father, Zeke, Otto and George. In 1927 the brothers got together and formed a hillbilly band called **Ott's Woodchoppers**, the name signifying the family's former occupation. Willard played the fiddle for the band until shortly before his death in 1933. He was replaced for a time in the band by William Dingler, a fiddler influenced by Fred Woodhull. When Dingler left the band to form his own family band, Milo became the lead fiddler. Throughout the 1930s and 1940s the **Woodchoppers** played clubs, Granges, dance halls and were featured on Station WESG out of Elmira.

Milo Kouf, born around the turn of the century, toured the central NY area with the Woodchoppers until after WWII. He then ran an auto parts business and found time to play in two other bands, a rockabilly group called the **Boogie Masters** and a pop country band called **Sophisticated Country**. As late at 1977, Milo was still competing in the Newfield Old Time Fiddlers' Contest.

Elial 'Pop' Weir was born in Governeur, NY in 1890 where he worked as a lumberjack and learned to play the fiddle during slack times at the lumber camp. After moving to Hubble Hollow, near Cooperstown, NY he and his wife performed at house dances and dance halls, Elial on fiddle and his wife on piano. Twenty years after he taught his children what he knew about music, Elial was still taking first place in fiddle contests in Oneonta and Schenectady. He taught his son Dorrance to play the tenor banjo in 1931. Soon three other children Don, Les and Violet took up the fiddle. Another son, Hy, learned to play the mouth organ. Don was the most talented, but after he was killed in an airplane accident, it was left to Les and Violet to continue the fiddling tradition. Members of the Weir family have been playing for nearly all of the past seventy years. In 1995 the **Weir Family** was one of the featured acts at the Watkins Glen Old Time Fiddlers' Gathering.

William Dingler was born in Philipsburg, PA in 1895. His father was a fiddler and passed his musical skills and his fiddle on to his son. When William was seven years old his family moved to Elmira, NY. There William became acquainted with Fred Woodhull and Willard Kouf. When Willard died in 1933, William got his opportunity to play in a band, **Ott's Woodchoppers**. He played in the group from 1933 until 1940 when he left to form his own band called **The Carolinians**. Five of William's sons played in the band, Bob, piano and accordion, George, bass, David, accordion, Don, guitar and John, like his father, the fiddle. William divided his time between the band and his store until declining interest in hillbilly music caused the band to break up in the 1950s.

John Dingler continued to play the fiddle after the band broke up. For a time he went to Texas and played in a group call **The Chaparrals**. In the early 1970s he returned to New York to help his brother Ben convert their father's store to a country music bar called the 76 Bar. They formed a band called the **Ding-a-Lings** with John playing the fiddle or guitar, George on bass, Bob on piano or accordion, Milo Kouf, fiddle or guitar, and Denny Dingler, William's grandson, on guitar. A couple of non-family members were also in the band, Terry Carlisle, drummer and Shirley Fox , vocalist.

Lyle Miles was born in Springwater, NY on May 12,

1902. In 1905 Lyle's father moved the family to Hornellsville, now Hornell. Lyle began to play the fiddle at age ten. He had been exposed to the music of Fred Woodhull and wanted to emulate Fred's style. He sold packages of bluing to earn money to buy his first fiddle. When he heard that the fiddle was at the Wells Fargo office he ran to get it. He was so eager to play his new fiddle that he could not wait to get it home so he opened the package on the lawn of a nearby church. He later took a few lessons from Leonard Hefter of Hornell, NY and was soon playing for silent movies and house dances. He tried vaudeville in Buffalo, NY but was dissatisfied with it. When talking pictures eliminated his job at the movie houses, he formed his own band, **The Lyle Miles Band**. He played fiddle with Ken Pierce on piano and Lloyd Hegadorn on plectrum banjo. When Lloyd left the band to form **Hegadorn's Banjo Band** in 1927, Lyle soon formed another band he called the **Hornellsville Hillbillies** with Fay McChesney and Archie Thorpe. Though the band changed personnel over the years and grew to have six members at times, the original Miles, McChesney and Thorpe stayed together for the next ten years. The band, like other hillbilly bands of that time, followed the pattern set by **Woodhull's Old Tyme Masters** with fake beards, country clothes, rustic names and slapstick comedy. **The Hillbillies** were regulars at the local radio stations WLEA in Hornell and WMBO in Auburn in the 1940s and 1950s. They were also recorded in Alfred, NY by Fred Palmer in 1943. When the popularity of their kind of music began to decline in the 1950s, the band members realized that the end was near. They played their last job in Medina, NY on October 11, 1955. Although Lyle continued to play informally, he retired from music to divide his attention between his farm and the marine sales business he'd started.

Grant Rogers was born in 1907 in Walton, NY. His father Delbert was a railroader, stonemason and a fiddler of sorts. As a boy of eight Grant learned to play the fiddle from Sherm Yorks, a peg-legged fiddler from one of the local lumber camps. Grant was a contemporary of Thomas Mullen, another good fiddler in the area. In the 1940s a local furniture company asked Grant to form a band to play over station WVOS out of Liberty, NY. He organized and played in the **Delaware County Ramblers** band until about the time of WWII.

No history about the beginning of bluegrass music in this area would be complete without mention of Jehile Kirkhuff. Jehile was born in Rush, PA on June 16, 1907. He began playing the fiddle at age five and took lessons from George Graham, a famous local fiddler. Jehile began to lose his sight in early childhood and was almost totally blind by the time he was fifty.

Jehile Kirkhuff

The Susquehanna County, PA champion fiddler in 1926, Jehile was the Pennsylvania State champion in 1947 and declared the Champion Old Time Fiddler in a contest held in Texas in 1954. Altogether he won twenty-three fiddle contests. Although Jehile played primarily as a soloist, he did organize a band called **The Coonhunters** which played as far north as New York State.

Jehile was 31 in 1938 and living with his cousin William Brotzman when he married Lola Stover, a woman twenty-five years his senior. Lola was an accomplished piano player and often accompanied Jehile's fiddle playing. When Lola died after thirteen years of marriage, Jehile returned to live with William.

Jehile taught dozens of local fiddlers and knew about 5000 different tunes, In addition, he had composed a number of fiddle tunes of his own. Much of his fiddling has been taped for historical purposes by the Smithsonian Institute. When Jehile died on March 21, 1981 at the age of 73 about sixty people with violins showed up at his grave side to fiddle him to heaven.

George Bourne was born in Oneida, NY in 1908 and learned at an early age to play the accordion. Although he was not a fiddler, George did organize and lead the band **North Country Hillbillies**. Along with George in the band were Irving Flanders on fiddle, Eddie Kilson on guitar, and Clyde Matthews on bass. The band played on radio station WLBU in Canastota and WIBX in Utica. The fate of the band was similar to others of that era. It ended with WWII. In 1942 George toured the state with Bradley Kinkaid and played on radio stations WGY Schenectady, WHAM Rochester and WNBZ Saranac Lake.

Ken Kane was born on April 29, 1914 in Hartwick, NY. One of eight children, Ken married in 1942 and began to farm the old homestead. In his time he was a farmer, stonemason, wagon maker, millwright, electrician and welder. He began playing the fiddle for enjoyment and as a means of participating in the social life of the community. In addition to the fiddle, Ken also played the guitar, button accordion, concertina, piano, banjo, Dobro and mouth organ. Ken was a contemporary of Les Weir and the two often played music together, switching off on the guitar and the fiddle.

Charley Hughes was born in Oneonta, NY in 1935. Two years later the family moved to Milford where as a young boy Charley learned to play fiddle and guitar. After graduation from high school, Charlie met 'Barefoot' Bob Kinney who had a popular radio show over station WCHN out of Norwich, NY. Bob had moved from the Rural Radio Network out of Ithaca to Norwich in 1953. In addition to his show, he ran a hillbilly park at Echo Lake near Bainbridge, NY. At about that time Charley joined Kinney as his backup guitar player and fiddler and stayed with him for about a year. Charley soon realized that the music he wanted to play was more the current country style and he left to form the **Rhythm Rangers** band with Eddie Dadovich, Neil Ralston, Clayton Loucks and Johnny VanPelt. By 1957 Charley had formed another band **The Westernaires** with Charley on rhythm guitar, Johnny Van-Pelt on steel guitar, Ken Shields on fiddle and Dick Thompson on bass.

Here we have an example of one source of music which developed in two directions. The music that Kinney and Hughes played together was called hillbilly. When they split, Kinney's music took the path of bluegrass and Charley Hughes' music took the path of country.

There were dozens of hillbilly bands performing in New York State from the 20s through 50s, including the **Hornellsville Hillbillies** from Hornellsville, **Ott's Wood-choppers** from Ithaca, **North Country Hillbillies** from Oneida, **Rusty Reubens** from Wellsville, **Woody Kelly's Old Timers** from Perry, the **Trail Blazers** from Cortland, **Old Dan Sherman and Family** from Oneonta, **Lone Pine Ramblers** and **Tune Twisters** from Elmira. However, the undisputed leader in popularity was the **Woodhull's Old Tyme Masters**. Without a doubt the popularity of this band influenced the format of the hillbilly bands of that period by being copied over and over.

The music of the fiddlers and the local square dance bands of northeastern Pennsylvania and New York State from 1800 to 1950 included reels, hornpipes, jigs, waltzes and schottisches, many brought over to this country from Great Britain, Ireland, Scotland and Western Europe. A sampling of the kinds of songs played by the fiddlers and the hillbilly bands includes Ann Green, Arkansas Traveler, Belcher's Reel, Black Cat, Blackberry Quadrille, Brown Jug, Buffalo Gals, Bury Me Beneath the Weeping Willow, Cannonsville Dam, Captain Jinks, Chicken Reel, Climbing Up Them Golden Stairs, Devil's Dream, Durang's Hornpipe, Eighth of January, Fisher's Hornpipe, Flop-Eared Mule, Golden Slippers, Happy Bill Daniel's Quadrille, Haste to the Wedding, Irish Washer Woman, Liberty, Little Log Cabin, Jam at Gerry's Rock, Marching Through Georgia, McCloud's (McLeod's) Reel, Mockingbird, Money Musk, Nellie Bly, Nellie Gray, Oh, Susanna, Old Gray Bonnet, Old Missouri Waltz, Old Zip Coon, Pop Goes the Weasel, Prisoner's Song, Rakes of Mallow, Redwing, Rickett's Hornpipe, Ragtime Annie, Rubber Dolly, Rustic Reel, Soldier's Joy, The Girl I Left Behind Me, Turkey in the Straw, Virginia Reel, Wabash Cannonball, Wake Up Susan, Wearing of the Green, Wreck of the Old '97 and the Wreck of Old #9. A quick glance indicates that there are at least a dozen songs that continue to be perennial fiddle favorites at present day bluegrass festivals.

Note the conspicuous absence of the "Orange Blossom Special." At the turn of the century and for fifty years after that, the fiddlers of New York and Pennsylvania were suspicious and resentful of what they called loose-armed southern fiddlers. "The Orange Blossom Special" had been written in Jacksonville, FL during the mid-1930s by Chubby Wise and Ervin Rouse, two Southern fiddlers.

Songs about the local area inspired by natural disasters such as floods and storms were popular. Other songs told about railroading, canal building, dam building, logging, rafting and quarrying. Still other songs related grisly stories about local murders. Specifically there were songs about the Erie Canal, Cannonsville Dam, Springfield Mountain and the Berlin, NY murder of Mary Wyatt by her husband of one week.

There are three contemporary New York State fiddlers who have been playing from their younger days to the present. Mark Hamilton is an old-time fiddler from the Watkins Glen area. Larry Downey, born in the Binghamton area in 1910, is still performing onstage and giving lessons. Hilton Kelly from Roxbury, NY leads a square dance band still performing at the present.

There are also two fine female fiddlers who have contributed greatly to their respective fiddle organizations. Marjorie Crawford, of New Berlin, NY conceived and organized the Del-Se-Nango Fiddlers Association. For many years the organization has sponsored an annual square dance caller's competition in Norwich, NY.

Marjorie Crawford

Marjorie was instrumental in the purchase of the Silver Dollar Saloon in McDonough, NY by the Del-Se-Nango Fiddlers for use as a square dance venue. The Silver Dollar Saloon, renamed the Del-Se-Nango Music Haven, was also the site of several one-day bluegrass music festivals. Marge was very active in the organization until her death on October 13, 1998.

The second female fiddler is Alice Clemens of the New York State Old Time Fiddlers association. Alice, an excellent fiddler, was a charter member of the organization. She has served as an officer for many years and is a very active member of the group. NYSOTF has its Fiddlers Hall of Fame located in Osceola, NY.

Fiddlers reigned supreme in rural music-making from the time of the Civil War until the 1920s and 1930s. They played in farm houses and hay barns. Now their sons, daughters and grandchildren would play in square dance bands in dance halls and on stage shows through the 1940s and 1950s.

Hillbilly To Bluegrass

Three related happenings brought bluegrass music to New York and Pennsylvania in the 1920s and the 1930s. The first event was the invention of the phonograph by Thomas Edison in 1877. Although the first machines were primitive, by 1920 vast improvements made the purchase of records and the means to play them relatively inexpensive.

The second event was the development of the radio by Guglielmo Marconi in 1895. The development of the radio kept pace with the record industry and by 1920 there were scheduled and commercial programs on the airways. And by that time there was usually at least one home in a rural community where a radio or record player could be found and where neighbors could listen to their favorite recording or hillbilly program.

The last event was the realization in the South and to the West that fiddlers, brother duos, hillbilly bands and musician-vocalists were very marketable. By the end of the 1920s the people north of the Mason-Dixon Line were listening to those performers over radio stations WLW out of Cincinnati, OH, WLS out of Nashville, TN and WWVA out of Wheeling, WV. Northerners were also buying records featuring the music of these same performers issued by Edison, Victor Bluebird, Brunswick, Decca and a host of other similar record companies.

In the process of gathering material for this book over one hundred bluegrassers and bluegrass fans were interviewed. One of the questions asked was, "How did you become interested in bluegrass music?" Though some of the people answered that the music had been played and handed down to them by older family members, the greater percentage of them said that as youngsters they had heard such performers as Bill Monroe, the Delmores, Roy Acuff or the Carter Family on the radio. Many said they had listened to these or similar groups on records. Each of the following, and indeed hundreds like them, made a significant contribution to bluegrass music.

Roy Acuff,
(September 15, 1903 – November 23, 1992)

Roy was born in Maynardville, TN and joined the Grand Ole Opry in 1938. He was the first popular vocalist on the Grand Ole Opry which had, since its inception in 1925, featured only fiddlers and string bands. He is particularly remembered for his recordings of "The Great Speckled Bird" and "The Wabash Cannonball" issued in the mid 1930s. In 1939 he asked good friend Pete Kirby, better known as 'Bashful Brother' Oswald, to join his string band, the **Smokey Mountain Boys**.

The Bailey Brothers
Charlie Bailey (b. February 9, 1916)
Danny Bailey (b. December 1, 1919)

From Happy Valley, TN, the Bailey Brothers began performing as a duo in the late 1930s with Charlie on mandolin and Danny on guitar. Although they played over many different radio stations in the south, they never made any significant inroads with recordings. In 1947 they formed a band featuring 'Tater' Tate on fiddle and Hoke Jenkins on banjo. Tate claimed that no one he ever worked with, including Bill Monroe, could draw a crowd like the Baileys. The band broke up in 1954 although the brothers did play a few festivals in the 1970s.

The Blue Sky Boys
Bill Bolick (b. October 28, 1917)
Earl Bolick (b. November 16, 1919)

When the pair from Hickory, NC broke into the radio and recording business in the 1930s, they called themselves **The Blue Sky Boys** to be just a bit different than the many other brother acts performing at that time. However, like many of the other brother acts, Bill played mandolin and Earl guitar. They worked for a time for the Crazy Water Crystals company over radio station WGST Atlanta, GA. Later they added fiddle player Homer Sherrill to the act. The group recorded from the 1930s to the 1950s, disbanding in 1951, although, like the Baileys, they did play for a few bluegrass festivals in the 1970s.

'Fiddlin' John Carson
(March 23, 1868 – December 11, 1949)

Born in Blue Ridge, GA, Carson was one of the earliest southern performers to record. He performed over radio station WSB Atlanta, GA as early as 1922. In 1923 he recorded the famous "Little Old Log Cabin in the Lane" for OKeh. The flip side of that record was "The Old Hen Cackled and The Rooster's Going to Crow." The promoter thought Carson's singing was awful and printed only 500 copies. 'Fiddlin' John sold all 500 copies from the stage at his next appearance. He also recorded for Victor Bluebird in 1934. The Great Depression ended his musical career after 1934 and he ended his working days as an elevator operator at the Georgia State Capitol.

The Carter Family
A. P. Carter (December 15, 1893 – November 7, 1960).
Sara Dougherty Carter (July 21, 1899 – January 8, 1979).
Maybelle Addington Carter (May 10, 1909 – October 23, 1978)

Alvin Pleasant was born in Maces Springs, VA. Although A.P. did conduct singing schools for churches and fiddled a little, he was working as a fruit tree salesman when he met Sara, born in Flatwoods, VA. The two married in 1915. When Sara's cousin Maybelle Addington, from Nickelsville, VA, joined them in 1926 they became **The Carter Family**. The group began recording for Victor in 1927. Their second recording session included "Keep on the Sunny Side," "John Hardy" and a Civil War song called "The Wildwood Flower" which featured Maybelle's guitar picking. Unfortunately, the initial success of the recording session was diminished by the depression and the Carters were unable to take advantage of their record hits. Instead of touring or performing on the radio they stayed home, playing at schoolhouse shows for very little reward. In 1939 A.P. and Sara divorced. Maybelle, with her three daughters, Helen,

June and Anita, went on to form a new act called **Mother Maybelle and The Carter Sisters**.

Wilma Lee and Stoney Cooper
Wilma Leigh Leary (b. February 7, 1921)
Stoney Cooper (October 16, 1918 – March 22, 1977)

Stoney was born in Harman, WV and Wilma was born in Valley Head, WV. In the 1930s he was a fiddler for Rusty Hiser's **Green Valley Boys** at WMMN in Fairmont, WV. After the band broke up Stoney was hired by Jacob Leary to play fiddle in the **Leary Family Band**. Soon he and Leary's daughter Wilma became singing partners and were married in 1941. Thereafter they played for a number of radio stations including WWNC, Asheville, NC in 1947. They began recording in the 1940s, first for Rich-R-Tone, then for Columbia. Later they switched to the Acuff-Rose label. Their final chart record was "Wreck on the Highway." After Stoney's death Wilma Lee formed a bluegrass band which toured into the 1980s. Rudy Perkins of Tunkhannock, PA sometimes traveled with Wilma Lee and Stoney when they toured in Pennsylvania. They were impressed with his songs and recorded a number of them.

Vernon Dalhart
(April 6, 1883 – September 14, 1948)

Vernon, born in Jefferson,TX first recorded with Edison in 1915. He later went with Victor where he became the first hillbilly recording star to sell a million copies of a record, "The Wreck of Old 97" in 1924-1925. Other big hits included "The Prisoner's Song," "Blue Ridge Mountain Home," "Death of Floyd Collins," "Rosewood Casket," "Letter Edged in Black," "Maple on The Hill" and "Golden Slippers." He recorded most of these songs from 1926 to 1930. The Depression ended his career as a musician and he took a job as a night clerk in a hotel.

The Delmore Brothers
Alton Delmore (December 25, 1908 – June 8, 1964)
Rabon Delmore (December 3, 1916 – December 4, 1962)

The Delmore Brothers from Elkmont, AL are remembered for their pure harmony. In addition the brothers wrote and recorded "Brown's Ferry Blues" in 1931 and "Blues Stay Away From Me" in 1949. They performed on the Grand Ole Opry from 1933 until 1938. After leaving the Opry they were affiliated with a half dozen radio stations including WLW in Cincinnati, OH. At one time during the 1930s they were the most popular radio stars in the country. Alton wrote more than one thousand songs recorded by such diverse artists as Grandpa Jones, Glen Campbell and Bob Dylan.

Bradley Kinkaid
(July 13, 1895 – September 23, 1989)

Born in Point Leavell, KY, Bradley was as popular a country singer as Jimmie Rodgers from 1926 to 1930. He first played WLS, Chicago, IL in 1926 with a quartet. Soon after that he became a singer for their *National Barn Dance*. He traveled to a number of radio stations during his career including WGY, Schenectady, NY in the 1930s where he made a handsome profit selling song books and making personal appearances. He recorded for Gennett, Brunswick, Bluebird and Decca from 1927 to 1934. Although retired in 1963 he consented to record 162 songs over a four-day period. From these recordings seven albums were made on the Bluebonnet label. Kinkaid also appeared one time at Mac Wiseman's Renfro Valley Festival.

Uncle Dave Macon
(October 7, 1870 – March 22, 1952)

Born in Smart Station, TN, Uncle Dave was over 50 when his mule-drawn freight line was rendered obsolete by the newfangled Ford trucks. Having played the banjo since he was fourteen, he turned to entertainment and was one of the first acts to be hired by the Nashville, TN radio station WMS. Soon he was appearing on the *Saturday Night Barn Dance*, renamed *The Grand Ole Opry* in 1927. From 1924 to 1938 he recorded over 180 songs for every major record label. Called the Dixie Dewdrop by Opry announcer George Hay, Uncle Dave appeared on the Opry until only days before his death. He left his banjo to Dave 'Stringbean' Akeman.

Mainer's Mountaineers
J.E. (Joseph Emmett) Mainer (July 20, 1898 – June 12, 1971)
Wade Mainer (b. April 21, 1907)

Both born in Buncombe County, NC, J.E. and Wade were not just a brother act because they had John Love and Claude Morris in the band for their first Bluebird recording session in August, 1935. They gave a new and popular bluegrass style rendition of the old song "Maple on the Hill" along with thirteen other fine selections. When the band split up in 1937, Wade went on to form the **Sons of The Mountaineers**. J.E. stayed with Crazy Water Crystals at WPTF, Raleigh, NC organizing a new band that included himself, Snuffy Jenkins, George Morris and Leonard Stokes. J.E.'s band continued to play at festivals from the 1960s into the early 1970s. At the time of his death he was preparing to leave for a festival appearance in Culpepper, VA.

Lee Moore
(b. September 24, 1914)

Born in Circleville, OH, Lee was working as a vocalist for Buddy Starcher's **Mountaineers** when he met Juanita Picklesimer, another singer. They were married on November 15, 1938 and sang duets in the 1940s and 1950s. Lee achieved fame as Old Lee Moore, the coffee-drinking nighthawk, premier disc jockey for the WWVA, Wheeling, WV radio station where he worked from 1953 to 1969. In 1974 he made two bluegrass albums with Red Smiley's **Cutups** as his backup band. He is also well remembered for his signature song, written back in 1893, "The Cat Came Back." New York bluegrass fans remember him as a guest on several of Bill Knowlton's *Bluegrass Ramble* television shows from the early 1980s.

Jimmie Rodgers
(September 8, 1897 – May 26, 1933)

Born in North Meridian, MS, Jimmie became the premier country artist of the 1920s. At the height of his career no other performer could approach his popularity. His record sales were more than five times those of his nearest competitor. Diagnosed with tuberculosis, Jimmie quit his railroading job and went to work for radio station WWNC in Asheville, NC in 1927. In the summer of that year he recorded "Blue Yodel" which became one of the first records to sell over a million copies. Two days before the 'Singing Brakeman' died he was in the recording studio for one last session in order to improve his family's finances.

Arthel 'Doc' Watson
(b. March 2, 1923)

Born in Deep Gap, NC, and blinded from infancy, Doc learned to play a banjo that his father made for him. At age thirteen he persuaded his father to buy him a guitar. He soon became proficient on both. In 1960 he performed at the Friends of Old Time Music concert in New York City. He made such an impact there that he was booked into Gerde's Folk City in Greenwich Village. In 1963 he appeared at the Newport Folk Festival. In 1973 Doc won a Grammy award for Best Ethnic or Traditional Recording. At present he is still recording and performing.

The Monroe Brothers

From the turn of the century until the late 1930s brother duos and hillbilly bands with vocalists became increasingly popular with the audiences of the states north of the Mason-Dixon line. However, there was little overall uniformity in the music being produced. Sometimes the fiddle was the lead instrument, sometimes the banjo. At other times it would be the mandolin. Or a song could be sung with no lead instrument playing at all. For some selections the bands would have a single vocalist. For others, two-part or three-part harmony. In early 1938, however, Bill Monroe began to change all this.

The Monroe Brothers were no different from many of the other hillbilly bands performing in the 1930s. Birch was the oldest of the original three in the group. Younger brother Charlie (July 4, 1903–September 27, 1975) was born in Ohio County, KY. William (September 13, 1911– September 9, 1996) was the youngest child of Buck and Melissa Vandiver Monroe and was born in Rosine, KY.

Charlie and Birch both migrated north to Illinois in the late 1920s where they worked in an oil refinery. During their off hours they began to perform musically in the area. Charlie became the leader of the duo and played guitar and sang while Birch played the fiddle. Mother Melissa died when Bill was ten. When father Buck died six years later Bill went to live with his Uncle Pen Vandiver. In 1929 eighteen-year-old Bill went north to join his brothers. Although Bill would have preferred playing the guitar in the group, because he was the youngest, he was relegated to playing the mandolin and singing harmony behind his brother Charlie's lead.

The three brothers began playing for dances in the East Chicago area and were soon working over radio station WAE in Hammond, Chicago, then WJKS in Gary, IN. In 1932 the brothers and friend Larry Moore were discovered by Tom Owen and they began to play for the *National Barn Dance* over station WLS, Sears World's

Largest Store. In 1934 Birch left the group to work at a steady job in a refinery and Charlie and Bill teamed up with Byron Parker, 'The Old Hired Hand.' The makers of Texas Crystals, a cathartic patent medicine, soon sponsored their appearance on station WAAW in Omaha, NE. From there Texas Crystals moved them to station WIS in Columbia, SC and then to WBT in Charlotte, NC. There they were left stranded when Texas Crystals suddenly withdrew their sponsorship. At that point, the brothers simply switched to the competition, Crazy Water Crystals, and continued to play over station WBT. In 1936 the brothers were playing over stations in both Charlotte and Greenville, SC when they were approached by talent scout Eli Oberstein to make recordings for Victor. Some of their subsequent hit recordings included "My Long Journey Home," "Roll in My Sweet Baby's Arms," "What Would You Give in Exchange For Your Soul," "Nine Pound Hammer" and "All The Good Times Are Passed And Gone." In 1937 Byron Parker left the group and Charlie and Bill continued on together for another year. However, there was friction between the two of them and in 1938 Bill, at age 27, left his brother to try to make it on his own.

Bill Monroe

Bill Monroe was well prepared for his new endeavor. His mother and father had musical abilities and as a toddler he had listened to his siblings singing and playing. As a teenager he played guitar accompaniment to his Uncle Pen's fiddling. He had listened carefully to blues and rhythm as performed by local black musicians. He had in fact played backup guitar for Arnold Shultz, a local black fiddler who worked the mines by day and played for local square dances by night. Bill also had the opportunity to play mandolin behind one of the best guitar players and singers of that time, his brother Charlie. And he had worked hard to perfect his ability on his own instrument, the mandolin. Other performers said early on that Bill Monroe played more cleanly and faster than any of the other mandolin players of his time.

Bill formed a band called the **Kentuckians** immediately upon the split with his brother and traveled to Little Rock, AR. The group did not work out to Bill's satisfaction and Bill moved to Atlanta to try again. This time he was not in a rush to get exposure. First he would select a guitar player. Then would follow endless hours of practice and preparation. A young man named Cleo Davis answered Bill's ad for a guitar man. After two months of practice Bill declared the band ready. They were soon hired at WWNC in Asheville, NC to do a fifteen minute show called *Mountain Music Time* every afternoon at 1:30. The third member of the fledgling band hired was fiddler Art Wooten and the fourth was comedian, bones and jug player Tommy Millard. Because Bill's home state of Kentucky was called the Bluegrass State he named his band **Bill Monroe and the Blue Grass Boys**. When the band moved to Greenville in order to replace the **Delmore Brothers** at station WFBC, Tommy Millard stayed in Asheville and was replaced by bass player Amos Garen. Bill was well on the way to implementing those ideas that would result in his unique bluegrass sound.

By October of 1939 the **Blue Grass Boys** were ready to audition for the *Grand Ole Opry*. There is some doubt about what songs they played. Some say "Fire on The Mountain," some say "John Henry," others say "Foggy Mountain Top." But there is no doubt it was Bill Monroe's spirited and high-pitched rendition of "Mule Skinner Blues" which impressed the Opry members and landed the **Blue Grass Boys** the opportunity to play there regularly. Within a year he was making a record for Victor in Atlanta with band members Clyde Moody, Tommy Magness and Willie Westbrooks also known as 'Cousin Wilbur.'

In 1942 the band was composed of Bill, guitar player Clyde Moody, fiddler Howdy Forrester and a new member, banjo player Dave 'Stringbean' Akeman. When

Howdy left to join the Navy, Chubby Wise became his replacement. When Clyde Moody left the band, he was replaced by Lester Flatt in April,1945.When Stringbean left the group in September, 1945 one of Bill's fiddlers, Jim Shumate, asked a young Earl Scruggs to audition for the banjo position. Earl, already playing for **John Miller and the Allied Kentuckians**, declined. A few months later when he was free of his obligation to the **Kentuckians**, Earl called Shumate and an audition was set up.

Because he felt a replacement for Stringbean was not necessary, Lester was initially indifferent to hiring a new banjo player. However, he was singularly impressed when he heard Earl play. The speed, clarity and timing Earl demonstrated with "Sally Goodin" and "Dear Old Dixie" convinced Lester and Bill that Earl would be an asset to the band. Scruggs was hired. The band now consisted of Monroe, Flatt, Shumate, Sally Ann Forrester, Jim Andrews and Earl Scruggs. Before the next year was out the band would also utilize Howdy Forrester, Chubby Wise and Cedric Rainwater. Although they did not know it, history was in the making.

In 1943, in addition to radio shows, stage shows and recording sessions, Bill Monroe also organized a traveling tent show. Presented were such varied acts as individual vocalists, duos, fiddlers, gospel music, step dances, square dances, comedians and blackface. In all there were sometimes as many as fifteen employees traveling with the group. Bobby Osborne and Jim McReynolds were two young men among the captivated audiences of two of these tent shows sometime during the 1940s and the experience helped them prepare for their own subsequent bluegrass careers.

1945 to 1948 were the golden years of the band which was to represent, for many, the epitome of bluegrass music. **Bill Monroe and the Blue Grass Boys** set a style and standard for their competitors and imitators. The records and music they made during that period were prized, studied carefully and copied by many of the other emerging bluegrass bands including **The Stanley Brothers, The Osbornes, Reno and Smiley, Jim & Jesse** and a host of others.

Then in January of 1948, Chubby Wise left the band to go over to WARL in Arlington, VA. He was replaced by fiddler Benny Martin. Only days later Earl Scruggs left. His replacement was Don Reno. A couple of weeks later Lester Flatt gave his notice. Within a month, Earl, Lester and Cedric Rainwater formed their own band. They were soon joined by guitarist Jim Eanes and fiddler Jim Shumate. As an example of the uncertainty of band tenure, Eanes was, within a week, hired by Bill Monroe. In May Mac Wiseman joined Earl and Lester and the band's name became **Lester Flatt, Earl Scruggs and the Foggy Mountain Boys**. Again history was in the making.

Bluegrass buffs are somewhat divided as to when bluegrass music started. Some say bluegrass began with such hillbilly bands as the **Skillet Lickers, Possum Trotters** or **Ridge Runners** at the turn of the century. Others cite Bill Monroe's 1939 split from his brother Charlie. A third faction claims it was when Earl Scruggs joined the **Blue Grass Boys** in 1945. And a final group insists that it was when Lester and Earl started the **Foggy Mountain Boys** in 1948. It is safe to say that the majority conclude that Bill Monroe fits in the bluegrass picture somewhere.

Bill Monroe was in an unenviable position. On one hand, his band was so good that he was the envy of all his competitors. His style of music became the goal toward which all the other bands would strive. On the other hand, the bands which copied almost everything he did were the competition and it was this fact that caused Bill to harbor anger against certain individuals for years. Eventually he realized that the bands which emulated his style and music were actually paying him the highest kind of tribute and there came an end to his enmity.

Bill Monroe was not the only one playing bluegrass style music at this time. During the next twenty years many other performers made contributions to the genre. For example, in 1946 the **Stanley Brothers**, along with mandolinist Pee Wee Lambert and fiddler Leslie Koch reworked an old song, "Black Mountain Blues," originally called "The Lost Child." After changing the fiddle tuning they renamed the song "Black Mountain Rag." In 1947 Jim McReynolds began his musical career by performing on station WNVA in Norton, VA. Soon after, Jim's brother Jesse joined him and introduced cross-picking on the mandolin. When Art Wooten joined the **Stanley Brothers** in 1948 he brought to them the Monroe style of bluegrass fiddle playing.

Just as there is some difference of opinion about when bluegrass started, there is also conjecture about the first use of the word bluegrass to describe this kind of music. In the late 1940s and early 1950s, the word bluegrass began to be heard. Some critics say the term was used simply as an adjective for Bill Monroe's **Kentucky Blue Grass Boy**s. Others say the word was used to differentiate the faster, high lonesome sound of Monroe's music from the somewhat different hillbilly music sound. Still others claim the word described a new genre of music. An interesting story is told by Everett Lily, a Foggy Mountain Boy himself for a time. At festivals Flatt and Scruggs fans would request songs that Lester and Earl had originally performed with Bill Monroe. Because the fans did not want to offend either Monroe or Flatt and Scruggs, they would request a bluegrass tune rather than a Bill Monroe tune.

In 1948 bluegrass music got a boost from an unexpected source. Pete Seeger, a New York State banjo player whose primary interest was folk music, had been playing folk tunes on his long-neck 5-string banjo for a number of years. He decided to publish a mimeographed instruction book to share his interest and delight in the instrument. Since that time thousands of copies of Pete's *How to play the 5-string banjo* have been printed and sold. There is little doubt that this manuscript paved the way for the more modern how-to instructional books for all six of the bluegrass instruments by prominent pickers. The following year Pete formed the folk group **The Weavers** and went on to make famous the songs "On Top of Old Smokey," "So Long, It's Been Good to Know You," and "Good Night, Irene." Seeger and **The Weavers** were blacklisted from 1950 to 1967 for their leftist political leanings. Nevertheless, Pete continued to promote folk music and his views on the 5-string banjo.

In 1951 Bill Monroe purchased a country music park in Bean Blossom, IN. Here, successive bluegrass festivals have become increasingly popular and well attended. This was an important step in the history of bluegrass. It showed that music parks could become financially successful. Over the next twenty years similar music parks would spring up in Pennsylvania, Edgemont, Lenape, Dorney, Hibernia, Sunset and Cline's Grove to name a few. In New York State there was Echo Lake, Hilltop Park and Rainbow Park among others. These music parks became a stepping stone to the present day weekend festivals.

In 1952 Bobby Osborne's teenage brother Sonny began recording with Bill Monroe. Having mastered Scruggs style picking, he soon developed a characteristic style of his own. Also in 1952, Reno and Smiley began to record what would amount to more than sixty sides for the King Record Company. In 1955, Mac Wiseman headlined in Sunset Park in West Grove, PA. In 1956 Walter D. Kilpatrick became manager of the *Grand Ole Opry* and, over Bill Monroe's objections, invited Earl Scruggs and Lester Flatt to join the other members.

Also in the 1950s three young musicians formed a band. Because they started off playing calypso music, guitar players Bob Shane and Nick Reynolds and long-neck 5-string banjo player Dave Guard called themselves **The Kingston Trio**. Their break came in 1958 when a Capitol Record executive heard them play in a San Franciso club and signed them to a recording contract. Later that year they recorded "Tom Dooley." Although they were considered a folk band, they performed a great service for the makers of acoustic guitars and banjos and in a roundabout way they brought a host of young pickers into the bluegrass fold.

In the late 1940s and early 1950s a group of folk music enthusiasts gathered around the Washington Square fountain in New York City to play their kind of music and share musical ideas. They were primed and ready to give at least a part of their allegiance to bluegrass music. In 1955 at Sunset Park, Oxford, PA a one-day country and bluegrass music festival was held. Attending were Ralph Rinzler, from New Jersey, Mike Seeger, Willie Foshag, and Jerry and Alice Foster from New York. These five outsiders were seeking authentic bluegrass music since they had been on the fringe of it around Washington Square for the past few years. When they returned home they began to spread the news about a new and exciting kind of folk music and soon there were northern disciples in and around Washington Square. Among the players were banjoists Tom Paley, Roger Sprung and Marshall Brickman, Harry West, mandolin and Eric Weissberg, guitar. Other enthusiastic disciples were Billy Faier, Arthur Jordan Field and John Lomax, who with his son Alan was recording folk music for the Library of Congress.

In 1957 Wade and Wiley Birchfield founded Wayside Records. Together with Frank Wakefield they produced two records that were later listed in the trades as 'Music, Bluegrass Style.' In 1958 the **Greenbriar Boys** became the first Northern band to compete at the Union Grove festival in North Carolina. At the time the band consisted of John Herald on guitar, Bob Yellin on banjo, and Paul Prespitino on mandolin. Prespitino was later replaced first by Eric Weissberg, then by Ralph Rinzler. In 1960 the group with Ralph Rinzler won first place at Union Grove in the old-time band contest. In addidtion to the **Greenbriar Boys**, another New York City group began to bring bluegrass to the North. Mike Seeger, John Cohen and Tom Paley, performing as the **New Lost City**

-40-

Ramblers, made some recordings of music taken from the bluegrass style of southern music from 1925 to 1942. Their music is considered pre-bluegrass by some critics.

In 1959 Alan Lomax promoted a Carnegie Hall concert that featured a potpourri of blues, country, folk and bluegrass music. Bill Monroe was Lomax's first choice. When Monroe expressed disinterest, Flatt and Scruggs were considered. Unfortunately they were unable to perform on such short notice, so **Earl Taylor and the Stoney Mountain Boys** were given the nod. Judging from the applause and audience response, they were the hit of the entire evening. Earl later commented that the audience reception was so great there would be five minutes of applause at the end of a song before they could begin the next one. Also in 1959 bluegrass appeared for the first time at the Newport, Rhode Island July 4th Festival. The show included **The Kingston Trio, Earl Scruggs, Hylo Brown** and **The Stanley Brothers**.

With all this enthusiastic interest in the five-string banjo, the Bill Monroe style of fast fiddle and mandolin playing and the high lonesome sound, players and bands were in need of places to meet where they could share their common interests in this new kind of music and indulge in the exchange of musical ideas. Local festivals within easy driving distance would become the answer to this need. In New York and Pennsylvania these early festivals would precede the beginning and organization of local bluegrass clubs by only a few years.

Prior to 1961 the music park festivals offered a mixture of hillbilly, country, old timey, fiddle, blues, folk and bluegrass music. On July 4th, 1961, Bill Clifton promoted a festival at Oak Leaf Park in Luray, northern Virginia, memorable because it was the first time a program consisted entirely of bluegrass music. Appearing were **The Country Gentlemen, Jim and Jesse, Mac Wiseman, The Stanley Brothers, Bill Monroe**, and **Bill Clifton**. The festival was memorable for several other reasons. Although invited, Flatt and Scruggs declined because they would not appear on the same stage show as Bill Monroe. During Monroe's performance he invited a number of former sidemen to play on stage with him. This invitation segment would become a mainstay at other, later festivals. Finally, at this festival there was a departure from the tacit agreement not to speak of the competition from the stage. Bill Monroe made a few joking remarks about Flatt and Scruggs. He also conceded that his, perhaps most famous gospel number, "What Would You Give in Exchange for Your Soul," was first performed by him and his brother Charlie.

The year 1962 saw the production of several exclusively bluegrass albums. In March 1963 Bill Keith became the first banjo player from the North to join Bill Monroe's band. Monroe was impressed by Keith's ability to play the old fiddle tunes note for note in his somewhat chromatic and syncopated style. Keith had previously played in a band called **The Kentuckians** with Red Allen and Frank Wakefield. When Monroe offered Keith the banjo job with the **Blue Grass Boys**, Ralph Rinzler, Bill Monroe's new manager, had a problem as Del McCoury was Monroe's current banjo player. The problem was resolved by switching Del to the guitar and lead singing role while Keith took over on banjo. Keith's first name was another problem. There could be only one Bill in the band. When Monroe found that Keith's middle name was Bradford, for the eight months while he was with Bill Monroe, Bill Keith became Brad Keith.

The first three-day festival with all bluegrass music was held September 3-5, 1965 at Roanoke, VA with about a thousand fans in attendance. Carlton Haney, a bluegrass visionary, produced this festival and offered some variations which would for the most part become tradition over the next thirty years. The festival featured contests, workshops, gospel on Sunday and a program built around Bill Monroe and former sidemen and their bands. Monroe was featured in what was called *The Bluegrass Story*, a musical chronology of Bill Monroe, 1939-1965. Former

Monroe band members took turns on stage with Monroe recreating the songs they had recorded with him. Conspicuously missing were Lester Flatt and Earl Scruggs.

This modest beginning preceded the emergence of a few three-day festivals and each passing year increased their numbers. In the early 1970s the number of bluegrass festivals in northeastern Pennsylvania and New York could be counted on the fingers of one hand. Twenty years later there would be scores of them.

Television and Film

In addition to those factors already presented, two other influences, television and film, certainly contributed to the growth of bluegrass music in the area under discussion. Until the late 1960s bluegrassers and fans could experience bluegrass via radio programs, records and music parks. One had to be persistent to find a radio station that featured bluegrass music. And although records were available, distances of several hundred miles had to be traveled to get to a festival to hear live performances. Local bluegrass enthusiasts sought exposure closer to home.

In the fall of 1962, CBS aired the first television show to use bluegrass music exclusively as background music. *The Beverly Hillbillies* theme song, "The Ballad of Jed Clampett" was written by Lester Flatt and Earl Scruggs although Jerry Scroggins was selected by the producers to sing it. By 1963 the song was number one on the country charts. Banjo players everywhere began to copy Earl's rendition and banjo sales throughout the country soared. Lester and Earl did make several guest appearances on the program from 1962-1968 and Lester performed his Granny dance each time. The two also introduced their song "Pearl, Pearl, Pearl" on the show. The program ran until 1971 and long after in reruns.

The success of *The Beverly Hillbillies* spawned two other rural situation comedies, *Petticoat Junction*, 1963 to 1970 and *Green Acres*, 1965 to 1971. Flatt and Scruggs also recorded the theme songs for these two programs.

Another television program, *The Andy Griffith Show*, occasionally featured Doug Dillard's bluegrass band. A young banjo player, Doug Dillard, and his guitar playing brother Rodney had been playing bluegrass part time in the St. Louis, MO area in the mid-1950s. With mandolinist Dean Webb and bassist Mitch Jayne they left for California in the fall of 1962 to become full time professional musicians. In November they were heard playing in the lobby of the Ash Grove folk club in Los Angeles and were quickly signed by Elektra records.

A publicity release by the record company led to an audition for the *Andy Griffith Show* where they made a number of appearances from 1963-1965. Their appearances on the show gained them a cult following. Will Geer played the part of their garrulous father, Pa Darling. The boys adapted to the role of reticent and backward hayseeds, showing little or no expression except when they were playing bluegrass music, usually accompanied by Griffith on rhythm guitar. When VCRs became household affordable, many of the Dillards' fans began to tape only the episodes that featured the Darling family.

Television was not the only medium to utilize bluegrass music. Forty years earlier Lyle Miles played his fiddle to accompany silent movies, a job he lost with the advent of talking pictures. In the 1960s, the music of the fiddle, banjo and guitar would return to the movies in the form of bluegrass.

In 1961 Joe Anderson, a film director in the Photography Department at Ohio State University, produced a five-minute movie. *Football as it is played today* used time-lapse techniques to give jerky action to footage taken at various Ohio State football games. The film, intended to be humorous, was to include a soundtrack featuring jazz or bluegrass music. Anderson and his graduate assistant John Szwed, who was a jazz musician, had difficulty matching the recorded sounds of "Dallas Rag" and/or "Foggy Mountain Breakdown" to the filmed action. They were joined by Franklin Miller, a senior at nearby Oberlin College, whose father knew and had worked with Anderson. Miller was a bluegrasser who had played in a band called **The Plum Creek Boys** at the Osbornes' 1960 Antioch concert. When Miller heard Sid Campbell's band **The Country Cutups** playing at a local hillbilly bar, he convinced Szwed and Anderson to listen to their music live. A short time later, the **Cutups** with Sid Campbell on guitar, Ross Branham on banjo, Bill Moore on fiddle, Dan Milhon on Dobro, Chuck Cordle on bass and Miller on mandolin, cut the soundtrack for the film.

In the following years there were several other successful attempts to use bluegrass music for background music. One was *Cheers*, a basketball game film that featured **The Country Gentlemen** on the soundtrack.

Two full length major films played their part in bringing bluegrass music to public notice. In 1967 Warren Beatty produced and starred in the film *Bonnie and Clyde*. Beatty had originally asked Earl Scruggs to write the musical score. He later called to inform Earl that he had picked the 1949 recording of "Foggy Mountain Breakdown" for the main theme of the background music. This was the first use of bluegrass music in a full length movie. Although Doug Dillard and Glen Campbell, along with a tenor banjoist and a fiddler, provided other bluegrass music for some of the chase scenes in the middle of the movie, it was "Foggy Mountain Breakdown" which benefited from the film when it became an instant pop hit.

Deliverance was the second major film to utilize bluegrass music, although in a different way. "Dueling Banjos" was a major part of the film and has an interesting history worth relating. Sometime prior to 1955 Arthur 'Guitar Boogie' Smith, not Arthur 'Fiddlin' Smith, wrote a tune called "Feuding Banjos". With Don Reno playing the 5-string and Smith on the tenor banjo, the tune was recorded in 1955. Public acceptance was unremarkable.

In 1957 the tune was revived as "Mocking Banjo" by Carl Story and the Brewster Brothers and recorded by

Mercury-Starday. For this recording the duel featured the mandolin and banjo. The Brewsters copyrighted this version with Starday as the publisher.

The Dillards band, featuring Doug on banjo, Dean Webb on mandolin, Rodney on guitar and Mitch Jayne on bass, recorded their version of the instrumental in 1963, calling it "Duelin' Banjo." Having adapted the tune and rearranged it, the Dillards also secured a copyright on the Elektra recording.

Except for an unusual chain of circumstances the tune might have had its short run of mediocre popularity and then been relegated to the archives, listed somewhere under the history of bluegrass music. However, in 1970 Houghton Mifflin published *Deliverance*, a novel by James Dickey. Hollywood took an interest in the book and prepared to release the movie version in 1972.

Previous films had used bluegrass music only as background. However, in the film *Deliverance* the performers and their music became a part of the action. The book describes Drew's picking "Wildwood Flower" on his Martin guitar joined by Lonnie, a local slow-witted youngster playing a 5-string banjo. The film version interprets the scene differently. To symbolize the conflict between urban and rural, sophisticated and primitive, and possibly even the mundane and the unchartered, the simpler tune is replaced by "Dueling Banjos."

It is rumored that Ronny Cox, the actor who portrayed Drew, was given the opportunity to do his own guitar picking for this scene. He declined and two New York City-based musicians, Eric Weissberg on banjo and Steve Mandell on guitar, recorded "Dueling Banjos" for the film. Weissberg and a different guitar player, Marshall Brickman, recorded other sections of the soundtrack.

Thus, the adoption of bluegrass music in film and television played a major role in the spread of Bill Monroe's new and exciting music.The time was now ripe for the pickers of the North to jump on the bluegrass bandwagon.

Organizations

After attending festivals in the late 1960s and early 1970s small groups of bluegrassers began to meet in their homes to jam. From these small gatherings grew irregularly scheduled jam sessions. When attendance began to approach fifteen or twenty people, someone would suggest formalizing the group. This resulted in the formation of an association, league or club, with a constitution, officers, dues, newsletters and sometimes the sponsorship of a festival. Although a few of these organizations, for one reason or another, eventually disbanded, most of them grew and flourished. This progression is evident in the New York and northeastern Pennsylvania organizations listed below.

New York State Organizations

Adirondack Bluegrass League (ABL)

Like many other New York State and Pennsylvania bluegrass organizations, the Adirondack Bluegrass League (ABL) was started by a handful of acquaintances who were eager to learn about and promote bluegrass music. Four of those charter members were Hank and Irene Clothier and Don and Berta Towers. Hank worked for Niagara Electric for thirty-eight years before retiring. He recalls much of what prompted him and Irene to get involved with the bluegrass movement.

"My first inkling that there was such a thing as bluegrass music was probably in the mid-50s when I was about thirty years old. From my earlier years I had developed an interest in country music, called hillybilly at the time, but my contact with it was very sparse. There were no musicians in my family/relatives that could have any connections with country music, so as the time went by it became sort of a background thing.

"To me, bluegrass came on the scene as a few short notes from the fiddle and banjo, a five-string gem I had never heard before. Finally, as months passed, I heard a bonafide bluegrass band broadcast on the [public address system] in a theme park and I was hopelessly hooked. At one point I had even considered buying a five-string banjo and luckily for bluegrass music, I decided not to.

"Along this period of time I met Irene and found that she liked country music and also could sing. She learned auto harp and we started singing old country and bluegrass songs. A real point of inspiration was a trip to Maine to meet the **Blue Mt. Boys**, a fine group of pickers in the Portland area.

"Down the road in the mid-60s we started going to the Berryville bluegrass festival in Vermont, because that was the only one we knew of. It was there that the idea of a bluegrass organization was hatched. Picture leaving a huge bluegrass festival area on a Sunday afternoon for a long drive home. As you pass the stage, there performing is Bill Monroe and Mother Maybelle together. A lot of thought for starting some bluegrass nearer home!

"After checking with friends on the idea of starting an organization there was enough interest to try it. On a cold, icy, winter evening [in December, 1972,] fourteen people attended a meeting [at the Masonic Hall in Hudson Falls, NY] and the ABL was formed.

Don and Berta Towers of Corinth were also a part of the growing bluegrass interest and ABL movement in the area. They had promoted one-day indoor fests with bluegrass bands that included **Mac Wiseman** at the

Emergency Squad Building in Corinth in 1970 and 1971. Along with Don and Berta who assisted Smokey Greene with the 1972 weekend festival at the Don Boggs farm in Corinth, the ABL also helped out with work details and limited sponsorship.

Early ABL meetings usually included a jam session and a pot luck supper. Attendance and membership increased. At some point in the early 1970s, the ABL began having picnics at the Schroon Valley Campgrounds, Schroon Lake, NY. After a couple of years the members decided that these picnics could become festivals and that revenue could be generated to promote ABL activities. The festivals became known as the ABL Roundup and are held each year on the weekend following Memorial Day.

After several years at Schroon Lake, the festival was moved to McChonchie's Heritage Acres in Galway. The proceeds from the roundup are used to promote monthly winter shows and other organization functions.

Current officers are President–Irene Clothier, Vice-President–Bernie Siegel, Secretary–Debbie Smith, Treasurer–Tammy Corwin, and Membership–Carol Rumpf. Board members are Hank Clothier, Chan Goodnow, Gene Reynolds, Daryl Smith, and Ed and Pauline Spires. Regular meetings are held on the 3rd or 4th Sunday of each month from September through May at the KFC Hall in Corinth, NY.

Central New York Bluegrass Association (CNYBA)

The CNYBA was started about 1975 in the Cato, NY area by a group who wanted to promote bluegrass music. Frank Saplin conceived the idea of starting an association and in December 1975 Dick Weldon, a member of Cato Lodge #141 offered the rooms at the Masonic Temple for the first meeting to discuss forming an association. A steering committee consisting of J.W. Allen, Bud Artlip, Dick DeNeve, Mark Hutchins, Frank Saplin and P. G. Skinner was formed. The members met every two weeks for the next three months to complete a six-page constitution which was duly ratified. The first officers were President–J. W. Allen, Vice-President-Terry Lee, Secretary-P.G.Skinner, Treasurer–Bud Artlip. Board members were Dick DeNeve, Marc Hutchins, Bill Knowlton, Frank Saplin, Dave Stevenson and Norma Sweet. Over the years past presidents have included Bud Artlip, Kay Betts, Don Dear, Drew French, Pat Garrighan, George Hall, Bill Holden, Betty Hoysic, Dick DeNeve, Bob Treat and Marv Warren.

Since 1976 CNYBA activities have included incorporation, producing newsletters, hosting pancake suppers and promoting festivals. Fred Lewis and Bill Knowlton were the organization's first honorary members. They were soon followed by Bud Artlip, Pete Carr, Dave Cleaveland, Chuck and Sharon Foultz, Bob Klaben, Dick DeNeve, Bill Rinker, The Salmon River Boys, Frank Saplin, Norma 'Granny' Sweet, Wayne and Sherry Thurston, Sharon Volles and Dick and Helen Weldon.

In the fall of 1976 the organization hosted its first mini jam which led to regularly scheduled repeats the fourth Sunday of each month from September through May. To raise money for club activities dues were collected and various items sold. In 1978 Pete Carr became treasurer, a job he's held to the present.

In February of 1978 CNYBA held its first big time concert at the Holiday Inn West, featuring Headin South and J.D. Crowe. Later that year they sponsored a Bill Harrell concert. There was a 10th year celebration at the K of C Hall in Baldwinsville, NY with music furnished by the **Salmon River Boys** and **Bill Harrell and The Virginians.** Current officers are President–Ed Campbell, Vice-President–Helen Weldon, Secretary–Thayle A. Phair, Treasurer–Pete Carr and Acting Secretary–Suzanne Privett. Board members are Mary Carr, Ray Crouch, Bob Klaben, Jerry Miller, Andre Revutsky and Carl Stump.

Meetings are held the second Sunday of each month at the Cato Masonic Lodge in Cato, NY. Mini jams are held at various locations in the area on the fourth Sunday of each month. From 1995 through 1998 the organization helped sponsor Bill Knowlton's Bluegrass Ramble Picnic Festival. The organization will hold their own festival in Lafayette, NY July 30-August 1, 1999. Newsletter editor Thayle Phair mails letters to 285 members each month. Records show about 325 current members.

Champlain Valley Bluegrass and Old Time Music
Association (CVB&OTMA)

This organization meets the first Sunday of the month at the Trading Post in Crown Point. Current officers are President – Joyce Cruickshank and Secretary-Treasurer –Alice Rydjeski.

Del-Se-Nango Fiddler's Association

This association was started by Marjorie Crawford on August 20, 1978 in New Berlin, NY. The name is derived from the three counties its membership includes, Delaware, Otsego and Chenango. It is a non-profit organization dedicated to furthering fiddle music in the area. Over the years the group has sponsored fiddle jams, square dance calling contests and bluegrass festivals.

In 1990 the Fiddlers performed at the Capitol Theater in Wheeling, West Virginia for Doc and Chickee Williams' 50th wedding anniversary. The music was broadcast live over station WWVA out of Wheeling.

Del-Se-Nango Old Tyme Fiddlers

High Peaks Bluegrass League (HPBL)

The HPBL was originally started in 1973 by Fred and Val Warner but was discontinued in 1974. In 1996 Fred along with Steve Feinbloom, John Nye and a few others reorganized the HPBL to help promote bluegrass music in the Wilmington, NY area.

The league meets for jam sessions on the second and fourth Friday of each month at the Keene Community Center at 7 pm. There is also a meeting and jam session at the Wilmington Community Center one Sunday of each month from 1 to 7 pm.

Current officers are President–Cathy Moody, Secretary-Treasurer–John Nye. John also produces the newsletter. Board members are Steve Feinbloom, Tim Kingsolver, Cathy Moody, John Nye, Pete Richardson, Yannig Tanguy, Fred Warner, Shirley Warner, Lynn Williams and Ralph Wolfe.

Hudson Valley Bluegrass (HVB)

HVB was founded in Highland, NY in November, 1994 by **Break Even** band members Joan Harrison, Rob Bradley and Jame Kalberson, **North Country** band leader Mike Burns, and several others including Jim Conklin and Joyce Cullen. Current officers are President–Jeff Anzevino, Vice-President–Chris Scheu, and Secretary-Treasurer–Dolores Tubbs. Dolores is also membership coordinator. Board members include officers and Mike Burns, Joyce Cullen, Jim Romine, Janie Schoenbaum and Eric Spaulding. There are about 250 current dues-paying members.

The group hosts shows in the area at the Rhinecliff Hotel in Rhinecliff, NY, the Vassar Brothers Theater and the Cunneen Hackett Cultural Center. Presentations have included **Roger Sprung, Bill Keith, Gibson Brothers** and a Steve Kauffman workshop.

They also host a radio program featuring bluegrass, cajun and old time country music over WHWC Poughkeepsie (950 AM) on Tuesday from 6 to 9 pm. On September 18, 1999 they will host a one-day outdoor show with **Bob Paisley, Heinzevino, North Country, Salamander Crossing** and **Chris Jones** scheduled to play.

There are monthly meetings and jams on the third Wednesday of the month at the Pirate Canoe Club in Poughkeepsie, NY.

Kline Valley Bluegrass League (KVBL)

No information available.

Long Island Bluegrass League (LIBL)

In 1978 a bluegrass trio presented a music program at Stony Brook College. After the performance, several members of the audience stayed around for an informal jam. The members of the trio, Arthur Liblit, Evan Liblit and Ken Jewell enjoyed this informal jam so much they decided to form a bluegrass club, now called the LIBL. Originally they charged membership fees but soon discarded the idea of dues and a constitution as being too formal. Dennis Corbett is president of the club and does the occasional newsletter for the approximately 50 members. The group meets on the first Sunday of the month year round at Diamonds in Lindenhurst, Long Island. The number of people attending the meeting varies from 20 to about 40.

New York State Old Time Fiddler's Association (NYSOTFA)

The NYSOTFA began in 1972 and has as its purpose the preservation, promotion and perpetuation of the art of old time fiddling. Just a few miles north of Osceola, NY stands the Hall of Fame and Museum Institute which houses tapes, photographs, records, instruments, wearing apparel and scrapbooks.The museum is open on special occasions and every Sunday from Memorial Day to the third Sunday in October. Since 1976 the museum also displays a plaque for each individual selected as an outstanding fiddler. Each year the nominees for induction to the Hall of Fame are narrowed down to three and then voted on by the membership. Induction ceremonies take place at the Fiddler's annual picnic held at the Cedar Pines Restaurant on the last Saturday in July.

Old Tyme Bluegrass and Traditional Music Association
(OTBA)

Bill Massoth from Patterson, NY helped organize this bluegrass organization in the Schenectady area in the 1980s. It is now defunct.

Pennsylvania New York Bluegrass and Country Music Association (Penny)

In the fall of 1980 Randy Cornwell, Harry Hartz, Ken Oakley and Leo Strong from Deposit signed up for a 5-string banjo course. Taught by Gil Siegers at the Union-Endicott High School, Endicott, NY, the course lasted ten weeks and included weekly practice assignments. Trying to find a place to hold practice sessions, the four chose Jim Baudendistle's storage barn in Gulf Summit, NY. Practices were Thursday nights and Jim, with his old dobro, would often join in. Before the banjo course was over Jim had accompanied the others to Endicott to visit the class and hear a fine example of bluegrass music played by guests Larry Downey, Bob Lindsey and Gene Phillips.

By the time the class was over a few musicians, including Gil Siegers and his son Bobby, were appearing at the barn in Gulf Summit just to do a little picking. At that time the sessions were changed from Thursday to Friday nights and would continue from September to the end of May. In an area where people of all walks of life were taking an interest in bluegrass this weekly picking session soon attracted dozens of people from places like Owego, Unetego, Syracuse, Binghamton, New Milford and as far south as Scranton, PA. The original number of people grew to a dozen, then twenty and even more on some nights. A guest book appeared for all to sign and raffles were held to pay for the coffee and cookies Jim and Rita Baudendistle supplied.

Many of those who showed up at the barn were former Gil Siegers pupils. Some were accomplished bluegrass musicians and others were just curious observers. Included in that first group of pickers and guests were Gene Clayton, Juan Cornwell, Dennis Crawford, Butch Cross, Lee Cross, Ed Flynn, Joe Ganna, Marv Hall, Bob Hazen, Dane Helt, Billie and Wilbur Karcher, Clint Lainhart, John Larribee, Ray and Betty Lindsey, Harold Linkroum, Ernie Martin, Brian Miller, Cathy Pratt, Jim Pritchard, Gene Raymond, John and Char Thompson, and Dan White. Others who came a few months later were Rusty Carvin, Stan Coleman, Marge Crawford, Dave Denny, Barney French, Ray Fritz, Gary Harper, Bob Lindsey, Peter Plain, Patty Smith and Ted Wrench.

One Friday night in the spring of 1981, Ray Rogers attended a session and suggested that some of the members of the group begin to play out for such things as Windsor Firemen Field Days, Deposit Lumberjack Days, Susquehanna Moose Club and the Kellystone Park annual bluegrass weekend. In the discussions which followed it was decided to form an organization which became known as Penny since the members were from both Pennsylvania and New York. The first year officers were President–Ken Oakley, Vice-President–Gene Raymond, Secretary–Ray Rogers, and Treasurer–Lee Cross. Board of directors members were Jim Baudendistle, Butch Cross, Harold Linkroum and Dan White. Members Gene Clayton, Ed Flynn, Marv Hall and Billie Karcher volunteered to draft a constitution. The purpose of the organization as stated in the constitution is to promote country and bluegrass music, to donate to charitable organizations and to provide financial aid to local needy individuals and families.

In addition to those members already mentioned, the membership roster in August 1982 included Bert Baker, Tom Brown, Randy Cornwell, Dennis Crawford, Al Decker, Iva Gow, Tracey Hellwell, Geoff Kaufmann, Larry Kessa, Richard LaBarre, Gil Loveland, Lubeck Family, Michelle Miller, Marium Mitchell, Bert Moore, Liz Osada, Robert Rynearson, Gil and Bobby Siegers, Robert Silvernail, Bob Smith, Irene Thurston, Mike Toole, Tom Toole, Ben

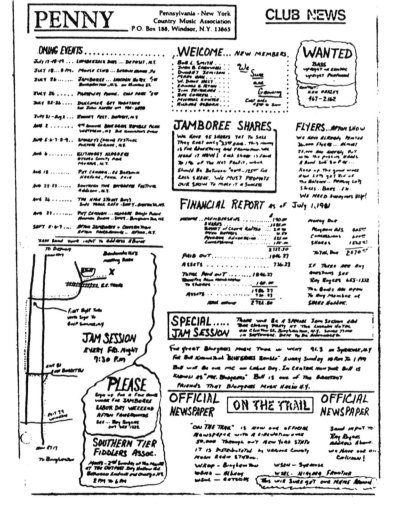

Penny's first newsletter July 1981

Stone, Tex Suttle, Sue Vanderbilt and Robert Vedder. At present there are about two hundred twenty members.

In addition to promoting the 1981 Afton Festival, Ray Rogers produced the *Penny Newsletter* for June, July and August of 1981. In 1982 Bob Hazen took over the job of getting the *Penny Newsletter* out to the members. Bob turned the job of producing the newsletter over to Gene Clayton in June 1989. Gene, Dane Helt and Clint Lainhart did the newsletter until June 1992. Ken Oakley and Carol Ripic then took over for about three years until June 1995. Gene Clayton has done the newsletter since then.

Past presidents of Penny included Debbie Clark, Juan Cornwell, Billie Karcher, Clint Lainhart and Dale Maxwell. Current officers are President–Ted Wrench, Vice-President–Bud Fish, Secretary–Billie Karcher and Treasurer–Pat Shultes.

Southern Tier Bluegrass Association (STBA)

While still in high school, Jim Hartman and friend John Sanford listened to 33 1/3 rpm recordings by **The Osborne Brothers, Flatt and Scruggs,** and **Reno and Smiley**. They liked the music and began learning some of the songs. While on a camping trip in 1970 with Charlie Hartman (Jim's older brother) they played and sang enough to entice Charlie to try learning to play the fiddle he inherited from his grandfather. Charlie became intrigued enough to attend a bluegrass festival later that year in Warrentown, VA. Following another festival at the Take It Easy Ranch in Callaway, MD, the men, along with another friend, Dick Cook, began playing together at every opportunity.

Charlie took his wife Pat and their four daughters to the Gettysburg, PA festival. Upon his return home he and the others began to think about having their own festival. Charlie described it this way.

"A festival being a good idea, we had a small one in October, 1973 at the Willard Morse farm. Our donations were like $30.00, our expense was like $400.00. Seeing that we made out like captured bandits we moved to the Duane Dennis farm in South Canisteo, NY. Better success this time but not much. Bluegrass was new to this area."

The Willard Morse farm festival and the Duane Dennis farm festival were one-day only affairs. Charlie, his brother Jim, John Sanford and Dick Cook performed on stage for these festivals as **The Tuscarora Bluegrass Boys**. In 1973 the band also became the promoters of a bluegrass disc jockey show heard Saturday mornings over WLEA in Hornell. The Hartmans' third and last individually sponsored festival was a two-day affair in 1975.

At about this time, the group began to meet at Charlie's home and started to think they might form some sort of organization. Plans were made to meet more formally at the Masonic Hall in Canisteo, NY. At this meeting on Saturday, March 20, 1976, the Southern Tier Bluegrass Association (STBA) was organized. Officers included President–Joe Coursey, Vice-President–Jim Hartman, Secretary–Tootsie Cook, and Treasurer–Walter Forshee. The thirty-one charter members were Ken and Bert Baldwin, Dean and Joanne Bartholomew, John Bly, Richard and Nancy Bowmaster, Tammy Caparulo, David and Elaine Coleman, Dick and Tootsie Cook, Nelson Dibble, Walter and Vesta Forshee, Charles and Patricia Hartman, James Hartman, Rensyler and Penny Jones, Dorr Kilborn, David Reagan, Earl and Sandra Reitnauer, Donald Saam, John Sanford, Elwin and Joyce Snyder, Ellis Spencer, Bucky Wildwood and Ronald Wilson.

Over the past twenty-seven years, STBA has held meetings, picking sessions and summer festivals. It has also sponsored many one-day events at local high schools and lodges. These have featured out-of-state bands as well as local musicians. The proceeds often went to local and national charities.

Since the first meeting in Canisteo the STBA has met in scores of places in the surrounding area. However, for the past few years the meetings have been regularly scheduled at the Tuscarora Elementary School in Addison, NY on the third Sunday of each month, except for July. Current officers are President–Lynn Bess, Vice-President–Bob Miller,Treasurer–Lucy Norton, Secretary–Ann Kelley. Current membership totals 191 people.

Stateline Old Time Country & Bluegrass Association Incorporated (SOTC&BA)

This organization was started in the Steamburg, NY area in 1993 by Dawn and Ron Allan, Peg Crowell, Dick and Betty Young along with a number of summer camping associates and friends. The group originally met at the Genesee Campground for their jam sessions but have since moved to the Cold Spring Fire Hall in Steamburg where they have meetings and jams the second Saturday of each month September through May.

Present officers are President–Dave Smith, Vice-

President–Ernest Weller, Secretary–Betty Young, Treasurer –Ernestine Slade. Board members are Vera Bliess, Lee Kenyon and Stella Weller. There are currently about 45 members.

In August 1995 the organization held its first annual summer bluegrass festival at the Cold Springs Fire Hall in Steamburg. The upcoming 1999 festival will mark their fifth festival.

Southern Tier Fiddler's Association (STFA)

This group was organized by Harold Linkroum, a fiddler who lives in Vestal, NY. They held their meetings from 1976 to 1980, first at the Inn on Day Hollow Road, then at the Pine Inn, Maine, NY. At their peak they boasted about 50 members.

Thousand Islands Bluegrass Association (TIBA)

TIBA was started in 1990 by Beth Bauer, Chuck Constantino and Jerry Knapp in Clayton, NY. They hold their meetings and jam sessions at the Caddyshack Restaurant in Clayton the first Sunday of the month year round. The club has at present about 76 members.

Current officers are President–Robert Reome, Vice-President–Phil Willix, Secretary–Jennie Fitchette, Treasurer –Maureen Bartlett. Robert also does the newsletter. Board members are Dick Bartlett, Evelyn Brand, Tom Drake, Millie Garceau and Bill Kinne.

The group hosts a three-day bluegrass festival each summer in Clayton. This year they will also hold two mini-fests at the Caddyshack Restaurant, one in March and one in September.

United Heritage Fiddler's Association (UHFA)

The UHFA meets at Legion Hall, Gowanda, NY.

Western New York Old Time & Bluegrass Music Association (WNYOT&BMA)

This association was started by Dave and Monica Armitage, Kay Brownell, Dick Crowley, and Hal Kibler, along with a few others in 1978. The group originally held their meetings at Elwood Ripstein's Pony Track in Folsomdale, NY. They now meet at Bennington Lanes, Bennington, NY at 2 PM on the second Sunday of the month. Dave Armitage is the current president. The organization currently has about 200 members.

Northeastern Pennsylvania Organizations

Allegheny Mountain Old Time Music Association (AMOMA)

This association was started in 1990 by fellow musicians and friends John Clark, Ken Kartwright, and Bob Shunk in the Coudersport, PA area. At present the group has about 75 members. They meet the first Sunday of each month at Laurelwood Inn, Coudersport, for meetings and jam sessions from 2 pm to 7 pm year round. There is a monthly newsletter written and sent out by Pat Chappel. Current officers are President–Bob Shunk, Secretary–Pat Chappel and Treasurer–Paul Herzog. To date the organization has not planned or promoted any festivals, although many of their members attend the STBA festivals.

Appalachian Fiddle & Bluegrass Association (AFBA)

The AFBA was started in the Bath, PA area in 1972 by fellow musicians Louie and Larry Setzer, Ron and

Verna Parsons, Ray Fogel, Lloyd Hampton and Andy Tomsic. Louie Setzer was the first president. With Andy Tomsic as vice-president, Larry Setzer as financial secretary and Ron Parsons as board chairman, the organization soon grew to hundreds of members.

The first meetings were held at Blueberry Farm in Bangor, PA. In about 1989 the meeting place was moved to the Edelman Sportsman's Club in North Belfast, where the organization meets on the second Sunday of each month from October to April for meetings and music.

AFBA held its early bluegrass festivals at Cline's Grove, then purchased the Mountain View Park in Windgap in 1989 where they now hold annual festivals in August each year.

Country Western & Bluegrass Shindig

This organization is promoted by Walt Laubach, Sr in the Jerseytown, PA area. The group meets the third Sunday of each month from September to May at the Jerseytown Community Center for the sharing of music.

Fiddlin' Around

Steve Jacobi is the force behind this organization dedicated to the preservation of old time fiddling. Started in 1979 the group plays benefits, concerts and square dances in the area surrounding Steve's home in Equinunk, PA. They have for the past few years held a fiddler's convention in the fall at Beach Lake, PA where anyone who wishes may perform. On October 8-10, to celebrate their 20th anniversary, the organization in conjunction with the Wayne County Fiddler's Association will present the Autumn Leaves Traditional Music and Dance Festival in Honesdale, PA.

Steve Jacobi of Fiddlin' Around

North Eastern Pennsylvania Bluegrass Association (NEPBA)

NEPBA was started in 1988 by Jim Hannigan, Ron Penska and Barb White. They issued memberships but did not have a newsletter. They held monthly jam sessions at the Keystone College in Pennsylvania on the first Sunday of each month from September to April. After about eight years the organization and jam sessions were discontinued in 1996.

Festivals

New York and northeastern Pennsylvania bluegrass enthusiasts grew impatient with the necessity of driving several hundred miles to out-of-state festivals. They wanted bluegrass presentations closer to home and friendly picking sessions gradually developed into more organized festivals. Most of these enterprises began modestly, with a few local bands. The few very large 1970s festivals like Nancy Talbott's Berkshire Festival in Duanesburg, NY were the exceptions. Through the 1980s many of these festivals grew to the point where they offered a lineup that consisted primarily of big-name bands. For one reason or another, a few of these festivals were either discontinued completely or reorganized with changed sponsorship and locale. At the present time both New York and Pennsylvania host dozens of summer festivals, ranging from one-day affairs with local bands to four-day weekend extravaganzas that include workshops, band contests and stage shows featuring mostly big-name bands. The following chronology includes current and defunct bluegrass festivals held in this area.

New York State Festivals

Smokey Greene Festival

Having hired nationally known bluegrass bands to play in his night clubs since 1964, by 1972 Smokey was eager to hold his own outdoor bluegrass festival. Held in Corinth it was called the Smokey Greene Bluegrass Festival. Bands that first year included **Eddie Adcock, Lester Flatt, Joe Val** and **Cliff Waldron**.

Smokey relates, "The first year was a howling success in every way but one. A good crowd showed up, the music was good, the weather was good, everyone had a good time. The only bad thing about it was when it came time to pay up. There just wasn't enough money to go around."

The ABL helped out with a sizable check and Smokey took the balance of the debt as a loss. Don Towers helped him out with the second Corinth Festival and this time they broke about even.

In 1974 Smokey moved the festival to Ft. Ann, NY and took a bath in more ways than one. The festival was nearly rained out and the loss was enough to require a mortgage on Smokey's home. He figured his festival days had ended. However, the following year Pete and Shirley Bishop encouraged him to give it one more try. This fourth festival was held in Saratoga and was followed by subsequent yearly festivals until 1981. Bands booked for festivals at Saratoga included **Crazy Elmer, Doc and Chickee Williams** and **Yodelin' Slim Clark**. Smokey recalls that in 1979 he and Pete split the profits. He also remembered fondly what he called his 'Sinphony,' the gathering of all the bands in front of the stage on the last day of the festival for a group performance. Started in 1975 or 1976 this practice lasted for about five years when interest waned.

Smokey moved his festival to the Washington County Fairgrounds in Saratoga in 1982 where he continued to hold them until the last one in 1989. One of the most unusual things he recalled happening at Saratoga was at the 1986 festival when on a rainy day, expecting no one to show up, he sold about 1000 day tickets.

ADIRONDACK BLUEGRASS LEAGUE
PRESENTS THE ANNUAL

BLUEGRASS ROUNDUP

JUNE 5 - 6, 1993

SATURDAY: 11 AM - 10 PM & SUNDAY: 11 AM - 7 PM

at
McCONCHIE'S HERITAGE ACRES
GALWAY, N.Y.
Exit 12 off I-87 (Northway) / 13 miles west on NY 67

LOTS OF MUSIC - FIELD PICKING
COVERED SHELTER - FOOD & FUN
A NICE FAMILY FESTIVAL

Tentative Listing of Bands:

ADDIE & OLIN	JOAN CRANE
ALICE'S HOMEMADE JAM	THE PARLOR BOYS
BACK PORCH PICKERS	SAPBUSH HOLLOW
THE BEAR BRIDGE BAND	SPARE PARTS
BLADES OF GRASS	SWEET CIDER
BURNT HILLS BLUEGRASS	TODD MOUNTAIN
CEDAR RIDGE	LEE MOORE
DYER SWITCH	... and more
BLUEGRASS REMNENTS	

ADMISSION at Gate: Saturday $10.00 / Sunday $10.00
Weekend ticket (includes free rough camping) $20.00
Advance (Postmarked before May 15) $17.00
Children under 12 free
Send check or money order (payable to Adirondack Bluegrass League) to:
Tom Benson, 19 Joseph Lane, Ganesvoort, NY 12831

(Times and entertainers are subject to change.)

FOR MORE INFORMATION CALL (518) 583-2356

FOR HOOK-UP RESERVATIONS (FIRST COME) CALL
(518) 882-6605

COME TO THE CHILI PARTY FRIDAY EVENING. (BRING A
DONATION FOR THE CHILI POT!)

ABL Festival Flyer

Adirondack Bluegrass League

ABL held several picnics at the Schroon Valley Campgrounds where music was played by those in attendance. The members of the organization decided to move the picnic to Galway, NY, calling it a Roundup. They hired a few bands, provided a sound system and held their first festival in 1973. They continued this festival at Galway for a number of years. Sometime later, the festival site was moved to Frosty Acres in Duanesburg for several years. In 1993 the festival returned to McConchie's Heritage Acres in Galway where it has remained to the present.

Some of the bands performing at the ABL festival have been **Addie and Olin**, **Alice's Homemade Jam**, **Back Porch Pickers**, **Bear Bridge**, **Blades of Grass** with Shawn Batho, **Bluegrass Remnants**, **Burnt Hills** from the Albany area, **Cedar Ridge** with Butch Ryan, Rick Moon, Ken Meyers and Frank Mahoney, **Sapbush Hollow**, **Spare Parts** with Gene Clayton, Clint Lainhart, Tom Richards and Ken Oakley, **Sweet Cider**, **Todd Mountain** and Tom Benson's **Dyer Switch**. On a number of occasions Frank Wakefield has appeared on stage for the ABL Festival with a band made up of local musicians.

Bluegrass Ramble Picnic

In 1973 Bill Knowlton was playing bluegrass music from 9 pm to 12 pm on Sunday nights over radio station WCNY, Syracuse, NY. Stations WUNY in Utica and WJNY in Watertown were also carrying the program. One night in January of that year Bill said on the air, in an offhand remark, "Why don't we get together and have a picnic somewhere?" Following that remark he received a number of letters suggesting ideas for just such a gathering. As a result of those letters, in particular an offer from Frank Saplin for the use of the VFW Park in Hannibal, NY, the first Bluegrass Ramble Picnic, a one-day affair was held there in August of 1973. The festival was well attended and the second festival was held in Hannibal the first Sunday in August the following year.

In 1975 the festival moved to Frank Saplin's farm in Meridian and the Ramble was sponsored by the Masons from Cato, NY. By 1980 the festival had moved to the Seneca County Fairgrounds in Waterloo where it continued until 1983, still sponsored by the Masons.

In 1984 the festival moved again, this time to the Erie Canal Village where it was held through 1986 and was sponsored by the Lake Delta Kiwanis Club. The festival was then moved to Town Lee Park just north of Rome. From there the festival went to Pulaski, NY where it was sponsored in the late 1980s and early 1990s by the Pulaski Lion's Club. Then it moved to the Oswego County Fairgrounds in Sandy Creek, NY, still under the sponsorship of the Lions. At some point during the 1980s the festival grew from a one-day event to a two-day, then three-day event with an open stage on Friday night.

In all those years the members of the Central New York Bluegrass Association were peripherally involved with the Ramble as helpers, ticket takers and attendants. Some of the CNYBA members even performed on stage as members of local bands. In addition to Bill Knowlton, members of the CNYBA involved in festival preparation included Pete Carr, Frank Saplin and Dick and Helen Weldon. In 1995 for the 23rd annual Ramble, still held at the Oswego County Fairgrounds in Sandy Creek, NY, the CNYBA officially became a sponsor. Their sponsorship continued from 1995 to 1998 with a change of site for the 1998 festival to Lafayette, NY.

At some point in 1998 the membership of the CNYBA made the decision to break from the Bluegrass Ramble Festival and hold their own, still in Lafayette the first weekend in August, 1999. However, the Bluegrass Ramble will continue as the 27th annual festival to be held in Little York Park just north of Cortland, NY on Sunday, August 1,1999 as a free, one-day event, very similar to the

Bluegrass Ramble Picnic at Frank Saplin Farm 1980

original picnic held twenty-six years earlier. Among the bands scheduled to play at this 27th annual are **Bristol Brothers, The Delaney Brothers, Lonesome Road Ramblers** and **The Salmon River Boys.** Over the years the Bluegrass Ramble featured local bands including **Andy Pawlenko and The Smokey Hollow Boys, Bert Baker, Cranberry Lake, The Delaneys, Fish 'n' Friends, The Fox Family, Gibson Brothers, Gold'n Blu'Grass** with Fred and Doug Bartlett, **Hal Casey, The Henrie Brothers, Joyful Noise String Band, The Lockwood Mountain Boys, Moonshine Hollow, Norma 'Granny' Sweet and Company, Redwood Hill, The Salmon River Boys, Seneca Turnpike, Spare Parts, Stump Hollow** and **The Tompkins County Horseflies.**

Southern Tier Bluegrass Association

Charlie and Jim Hartman with the help of friends John Sanford and Dick Cook held three festivals before the STBA was formally organized. The first was a one-day affair at the Willard Morse farm in 1973. The second was another one-day festival at the Duane Dennis farm in South Canisteo where Charlie, Jim, John and Dick performed as **The Tuscarora Bluegrass Boys.** In addition to this group, friends Dean Bartholomew, Kenny Bennett, Dick Bouck, Dick Bowmaster, Jim and Steve Davey, Deak King and Duane Dennis played on stage. They also helped promote the festival. About 150 people attended the 1974 festival. A local newspaper article reported that the Dennis farm festival was one of only sixty-eight bluegrass festivals scheduled for the United States that year, most in Virginia and North Carolina. The 1975 festival was a two-day affair. Bands included **The Bartholomew Brothers, Ozark Snyder** and **The Tuscarora Bluegrass Boys.** Admission was $3.00 for two days or $2.00 for each day. The following year, 1976, the people involved with these three festivals got together with some other local individuals interested in bluegrass and formed the Southern Tier Bluegrass Association.

The Hartmans had sponsored the three earlier events. Now the STBA would sponsor the festivals and with organizational support plans became bolder. The August 14-15, 1976 STBA Festival bands included **The Bartholomew Brothers, Bill Schweigert and Potter County Bluegrass, Catfish Quartet, Endless Mountain Green, Jim Davey and The Sounds of Bluegrass, Voices of Bluegrass** with Roy Matthews, Jeff and Marlene Wisor, Bucky Walters and Steve Walker, **Jim Sherwood and the Music Makers, The Pearson Brothers, Tuscarora Bluegrass Boys** and **Willing Boys**.

The fifth STBA Festival, 1977, was innovative because it featured a nationally known band, **Del McCoury**. Also appearing were **Border City** with Bob Schneider on banjo and the 1976 local bands. **Endless Mountain Green** included Ward Stout on fiddle. A local newspaper article stated, "This year there is at least one bluegrass festival somewhere in the United States every weekend during the summer months." It also noted that listeners were bringing lawn chairs to the stage area.

The Bluegrass Cardinals, another nationally known band, was featured for the 1978 festival. Also appearing were **The Bartholomew Brothers, Border City, Cayuga Bluegrass Works, Diamondback Rattlers** with Curt Albertalli, Marc Chevalier, Dean Goble, and Roy Matthews, **Jim Sherwood & the Music Makers, Night Watch** and **Union Hill**. This festival also introduced fiddle and band competitions.

Interviews and research revealed interesting facts about two of the bands that played that year. Roy Matthews explained how the **Diamondback Rattlers** got their name. Prior to their 1978 STBA Festival engagement, the band had worn black shirts with a yellow band around the front. Someone exclaimed the colors reminded them of a rattlesnake so the group renamed itself **Diamondback**

Rattlers. Secondly, The **Cayuga Bluegrass Works**, consisting of Bill and Maggie Anderson, Bill Forrest and Dana Paul, was one of the first bands to play at the Opry House in Bainbridge, NY.

The seventh festival in 1979 was the first one held at the Addison CB Campgrounds and featured **Joe Val, Whetstone Run, Border City, Cayuga Bluegrass Works, Cold Spring Bluegrass Band, Corning Grass Works, Diamondback Rattlers, Hard Times** and **Iroquois Country Grass.** The eighth, ninth and tenth annual festivals were also held at the CB Campgrounds. **The Doug Dillard Band** played at the tenth.

Diamondback Rattlers: Roy Mathews and Carl, Terry, Rod Kithcart

From 1983 through 1987 the STBA festivals were held at Hickory Hill in Bath, NY. Featured bands included **Bill Harrell, Fox Hollow, Jim & Jesse, Johnson Mt. Boys, Larry Sparks, Lost and Found, Spirits of**

Bluegrass, **Tony Trischka** and **Whetstone Run** with Lynn Morris. Local groups included **Bluegrass Express, Creek Bend** with Rick Schaeffer on bass, Mark Panfil on banjo, Carl Eddy on guitar and Ted Lambert on fiddle, **Dempsey Station, North Fork Alliance, Diamondback Rattlers** with Roy Matthews on banjo, Carl Kithcart on guitar, Rod Kithcart on bass and Terry Kithcart on mandolin and **The Spencer Mountain Clan** with Bill and Jolene Anderson. The 1987 band contest winner was a hastily organized pick-up group called **The Shady Mountain Boys** headed by fiddler Jim Wallace. When the winner was announced, Jim didn't realize they had won because he "forgot what the [band] name was."

The 1988 and 1989 festivals returned to the CB Campground. Featured bands included **Creek Bend, Dark Hollow, Jimmy Martin, John Rossbach and Chestnut Grove, Paul Adkins** and **Warrior River Boys**.

The STBA Festival moved to a fourth site for the 1990-1995 years, Thomas Homestead near Savona, NY. The 1990 festival may be noted for Ward Stout's playing fiddle for **Weary Hearts** with Lynn Morris. The following year brought the first appearance of the **Fox Family** at the STBA festival. The 1991 festival marked the first appearance of **Plexigrass** with Doug Trotter on guitar, Lance Trotter on bass, Carl Kithcart on banjo and Terry Kithcart on mandolin. At the 1992 festival, Dana Paul made another appearance, this time as bass player with **Cornerstone**, an Ithaca-based band. Also playing that year was the **Bluegrass Dinosaurs** with Bob Schneider on banjo, Mark Orshaw on guitar and Jeff Wisor on fiddle. The 1993 festival lineup included the **Case Brothers** with Dick Bowden on guitar and Bob Mavian on mandolin. Bob was a former banjo student of Ferris 'Kit' Kithcart.

The 1995 festival saw the first appearance of the local bands **Fish 'n' Friends** with Chris Brown on mandolin, Gene Clayton on guitar, Steve DiRancho on banjo, Bud Fish on bass and Kevin Whalen on dobro and

Rosewood Hill with Ken Hurlburt on banjo, Steve Lundberg on mandolin, Steve Tryon on bass, John Vaughn on fiddle and Tim Wallbridge on guitar. This festival also saw the return of the original **Diamondback Rattlers** with the same members as in the 6th STBA Fest in 1978.

The STBA returned to the CB Campground for the third time in 1996 for the 24th annual festival. Charlie Hartman on fiddle, and brother Jim on banjo, returned to the stage after a twenty year hiatus, playing in the **STBA Band** along with Bill Anderson on dobro, Jolene Anderson on bass and Ken Pierson on guitar. Other local bands included **Pasture Prime** with Andy Alexander on banjo, Sue Alexander on bass, Roger Bakehorn on mandolin and Jurg Butler on guitar and **Cedar Ridge** with Bob Hegedorn on fiddle, Frank Mahoney on banjo, Ken Meyers on guitar, Rick Moon on mandolin and Butch Ryan on bass.

The 25th annual festival saw the return of the **STBA Band** and an appearance by the **Lonesome Road Ramblers**, Stan Ink on banjo, Steve Lundberg on guitar, Mark Orshaw on mandolin and Steve Tryon on bass. Their use of a single voice microphone affirmed their belief in the 'traditional' approach to amplification.

Among the local bands at the 1998 25th annual festival were **Creek Bend**, **Diamondback Rattlers** and **STBA**. Making their first appearance at this festival were **Crossfire** with Joe Connally on banjo, Rose Connally on bass, Hank Runser on fiddle, Pete Peterson on mandolin and Ken Teats on guitar and **Stump Hollow** with Chris Pepe on banjo, Suzanne Privett on bass, Carl Stump on guitar and Lori Thompson on mandolin.

Berkshire Festival

In 1975 Nancy Talbott promoted the first Berkshire Festival in Duanesburg. It was one of the first big festivals in New York State. Nancy hired the biggest and the best bands including **Banjo Dan and The Midnight**

Plowboys, Bill Monroe, The Carter Family, Del McCoury, Jimmy Martin, The Osborne Brothers, Peter Rowan, Quicksilver, Seldom Scene, Tony Rice and Vassar Clements. She included Smokey Greene and a few other local bands as well.

Actually there were several other earlier sites for the festival in nearby locations, but for the final years the festival was held in Duanesburg. Nancy is proud to have been one of the first to bring big name bands to the New York area so that local fans did not have to travel hundreds of miles to see and hear a quality bluegrass show. Nancy said that the attendance for some of the Berkshire Festivals was in the neighborhood of twenty-five thousand. She discontinued the festival in 1985, citing competition and increasing costs as reasons.

Cleaveland Festivals

In 1940 when Dave Cleaveland was six or seven he heard Roy Acuff and Bill Monroe on the *Grand Ole Opry*. At that time he acquired a taste for bluegrass music. He attended a Smokey Greene Festival at Ft. Ann and both heard and saw excellent bluegrass bands. He quickly became enthusiastic about having a festival of his own. Dave's early festivals were one-day shows held in the Syracuse area and featured one or two bands.

In 1976 he presented **Joe Val and The New England Bluegrass Boys** at the Euclid Community Opera House using **Headin' South** as the front band. He followed in May 1977 with **Buck White and The Down Home Folks**. And in October of 1977 he featured **Smokey Greene** at Hungry Charley's in Syracuse. At that time Dave's son Perry made a guest appearance on stage with Smokey. Dave says he ran about thirty-five bands a year from 1976 to 1982. Job and family responsibilities cut into the festival promoting for the next 14 years. Then in 1996 and again in 1997, Dave held an outdoor fest at Otisco Lake. For this festival he hired local bands **Craig Parsons and The Blue Ridge Mountain Boys, The Delaney Brothers, Echo Mountain, Fish 'n' Friends, Grass Act** from Buffalo, NY, **Plexigrass** and **Rosewood**. In 1998 Dave's festival was held at Marietta, NY. Bands included **Blue Ridge Mountain Boys, Bosstone, The Delaney Brothers, Echo Mountain, Fish 'n' Friends, Now & Then, Pike Quarry Ramblers, Plexi--grass, Rosewood** and **Stump Hollow**.

Bridgewater Festival

Charlie Brown attended a number of one-day fests in the 1960s including some of those held at Echo Lake, NY. There he heard bluegrass music played by **Reno and Smiley, Jim and Jesse** and **Jimmy Martin**. In 1978 he decided to hold a festival of his own. He convinced the Bridgewater Fire Department to help sponsor the event.

For the following eight years he held festivals at Bridgewater using such out-of-state bands as **Bill Harrell, Bob Paisley and the Southern Grass, Del McCoury, Doc Williams and Chickee, Jimmy Martin, Joe Val, Mac Wiseman** and **Old Lee Moore**. He added a generous mix of local bands that included **Andy Pawlenko, Laing Brothers, The Lubecks, Moonshine Hollow, Smokey Greene, Spirits of Bluegrass, Traver Hollow**. Charlie would often make a guest appearance on stage at these festivals playing guitar or bass with local bands such as the **Lubecks** and **Andy Pawlenko**.

For the last festival at Bridgewater in 1985 Charlie enlisted the help of close friend Dale Maxwell as a co-sponsor. At that point Dale was bitten by the festival bug and decided to host his own. Moving the festival to Herkimer, NY and getting the backing of the Herkimer Fire Department, he held his own version of the Bridgewater Festival in 1986. Bands included **Andy Pawlenko, Bob**

Paisley, Bristol Mountain Bluegrass, Del McCoury, Delaney Brothers, Moonshine Hollow and **Smokey Greene**. As sometimes happens when a festival is moved to a new location the turnout at the gate was not as great as expected. Dale made the decision to try at least one more year. However, the 1987 crowd was not big enough to justify continuing.

Spirits of Bluegrass with host Charlie Brown

Del-Se-Nango Fiddlers

Under the leadership of Marjorie Crawford the fiddlers have held one-day fiddle gatherings at various New York State locations including McDonough, New Berlin and Windham. Their eighteenth annual square dance and callers contest was held in May 1998 at the Touch of Texas Dance Saloon in Norwich, NY.

Kellystone Park

Throughout 1940 to 1960 there were dozens of music parks in New York and Pennsylvania. The owners of these parks would hire a prominent country or bluegrass band to play for the day and then get a local band to front for the headliner. Examples of these parks include Hilltop in Waverly, Rainbow in Maine and Echo Lake in Bainbridge, all in New York. In Pennsylvania there was Edgemont in Allentown, Sunset in West Grove, Lenape in Philadelphia and Cline's Grove in Bath.

Melrose Kelly, owner of Kellystone Park in Afton, NY, followed the format of the music park theme by holding weekend, that is three-day, festivals featuring country bands on Friday night and Saturday morning and bluegrass bands on Saturday afternoon and Sunday. Kelly also tried at various times live radio broadcasts from the stage, fiddle and banjo contests, square dances, Sunday gospel hour and cloggers.

Interestingly, this was happening from 1980 -1988 when most other music parks had faded out of public interest. During the nine years Kelly held these festivals, featured bluegrass bands included **Cranberry Lake Jug Band, Dempsey Station, Mail Pouch Express, North Fork Alliance, Penny, St. Regis String Band, Stateline**, and **Susquehanna Hat Company**.

The country-bluegrass weekends were discontinued in 1988 because of smaller crowds, weekend competition with other festivals and increasing insurance costs.

Opry House, Bainbridge, NY

In 1978 the Jericho Arts Council renovated the Town Hall Opry in Bainbridge. Their ultimate goal was to provide a place for plays, concerts and other performances. In September 1981, Lee Cross became the booking agent for weekly bluegrass shows. He was aided in this role by Frank Svatek who left after a few years to pursue other interests. Because of the high heating costs in the wintertime the weekly shows were switched to monthly shows which ran from September to April and have continued from 1981 to the present. Originally the audience sat at tables on what is now the stage but as crowds grew larger the stage had to be used for the performers.

Evelyn Baker became secretary for the Council in 1979, a job she held until 1988 when she took over as president, a position she currently holds. When Lee Cross died on November 6, 1987 Evelyn also took over the job of booking the bluegrass bands. Although she did the booking for only a few years, she is the one who introduces the evening's performers. Since 1990 Bill Laing has done the bluegrass bookings for the Opry.

Evelyn Baker and Jim Treat, Scott Corbett, Ray & John DeLaney

Just as other bluegrass venues have a mix of big name bands and locals, the Opry has followed suit. The name bands have included **Boys from Indiana**, **Eddie**

Adcock, Gibson Brothers, Paul Adkins, Tony Trischka, Whetstone Run and perennial Opry favorite, Bill Harrell. Local bands have included Appalachian Strings with Bob Klaben, Cayuga Bluegrass Works, Cranberry Lake, Cornerstone, Counterfeit Bluegrass, Creek Bend, Delaney Brothers, Diamondback Rattlers, Fox Family, Henrie Brothers, High Street Boys, John Rossbach and Chestnut Grove, Laing Brothers, Lockwood Mountain Boys, Rosewood with Perry Cleaveland, Spare Parts, Stateline and Susquehanna Strings.

With an unbroken string of 19 years of continuous bluegrass programming through the winter months the Opry has done its part to promote good family entertainment and bluegrass music in the Southern Tier.

Penny Afton Festival

In the late winter of 1980 Penny member Ray Rogers convinced the organization that they should hold a bluegrass festival in Afton, NY. Front money was raised by selling 100 shares in the festival's profits for $35 a share. The festival was held September 5-7, 1981. Featured bands included High Street Boys, Lockwood Mountain Boys, Mail Pouch Express, Michaels, McCreesh and Co., Shiloh, Spirits of Bluegrass, Tony Trischka, Uncle Steve Crockett and the Log Cabin Boys, and the Penny Band, The Junk Yard Boys. The festival was a success in every way except at the gate. The shareholders received about thirty cents on the dollar for their investment. In the years which followed Penny would avoid running festivals in the red by getting the bands to play for free or for a nominal fee since the profit after expenses would be donated entirely to charity.

Penny Afton Festival September 5-7, 1981

The Laing Family Festival

Bill and Doreen Laing and Gil and Ann Laing held their 1982 and 1983 family bluegrass festivals in Bainbridge, NY. The festivals were sponsored by the local Chamber of Commerce. From 1984 to 1991 the festival was moved to Oxford, NY where it was sponsored by the Oxford Lion's Club. The festival returned to Bainbridge where the Laings took sole sponsorship for 1992 and 1993. In 1994 and 1995 they held the festival at the County Fair Grounds in Norwich, NY.

In addition to the **Laing Family Band** as hosts, the bands playing at the Oxford venue included **Appalachian Express, Bill Harrell, Bob Paisley and The Southern Grass, Boys from Indiana, Bristol Mountain Bluegrass, The Cardinals, Chubby Wise, Dry Branch Fire Squad, Kevin Church, Outdoor Plumbing, Spirits of Bluegrass** and **Whetstone Run**.

When the Laings returned to Bainbridge many of these bands continued to be featured. Others included **Charlie Sizemore, Eddie Adcock, Fox Family, The Osborne Brothers, Lonesome River Band, Paul Adkins and Borderline, The Reno Brothers** and **Warrior River Boys**.

At the new Norwich location in 1994 bands included **Paul Adkins, Rosewood** with Perry Cleaveland, **Smokey Greene, Thunder Mountain** and the crowd-pleasing favorite who has been featured at all the Norwich events to the present, **Gilbert Hancock and Friends**.

In 1996 the festival sponsorship was assumed by Lynn and Aileen Oliver and Al and Thelma Evans who have continued to hold the festival in Norwich to the present. Although the name of the festival was changed to Family Festival, the **Laing Family Band** still performs at the event.

Peaceful Valley

Arnold Banker, with the help of his wife and four sons, ran the Peaceful Valley campground in Shinhopple, NY. The campground is open from the first of April until about the middle of November. In 1981 Arnold promoted a country band weekend. Dissatisfied with the event, he tried what he called "Beatlemania" in 1982. In the words of his son Glen, "The crowds trashed the place!"

Seeking less destructive weekend entertainment, Arnold decided to hold a bluegrass festival. With the help of Will Lunn, the leader of the Oneonta, NY bluegrass band **The High Street Boys** and Lee Cross from Unadilla, NY, another bluegrass enthusiast, Arnold planned a weekend that featured a mixture of big-name bands and local talent.

The lineup for the first festival in 1983 featured **Ralph Stanley and The Clinch Mountain Boys, Boys From Indiana** and **Tony Trischka and Skyline**. Local bands included the **High Street Boys** and **The Spirits of Bluegrass**. Bill Knowlton and Lee Cross shared the emcee. duties. The crowd that year was estimated at about 500 people.

As the festival grew Arnold relied more heavily on the bigger name bands and over the years he had them all including Bill Monroe and Mark O'Connor. It's not unusual to see such featured acts as **Bill Harrell, Bob Paisley, Chubby Wise, Del McCoury, Jim & Jesse, The Lewis Family, Lynn Morris** and **Ralph Stanley**, all appearing on the same day. Arnold did leave a few open spots for such local favorites as Hilton Kelly for square dancing and Smokey Greene.

From March 1988 until the year of his death, 1997, Arnold hosted a midwinter weekend festival at the Pines Hotel in South Fallsburg, NY.

Arnold's wife Walburga and his four sons Glen, Louie, Carl and Arnold Jr. have continued the Peaceful Valley Festival, and in 1999 will hold the 17th annual.

Harry Grant Midwinter

Following the death of Arnold Banker in 1997, the owners of the Pines asked Harry Grant to manage the annual midwinter festival. When the Pines closed in 1998 the bands for the Midwinter Festival had already been contacted and scheduled. The management at the Friar Tuck Inn, Catskill, NY was agreeable to relocating the event to their facility. Harry Grant has successfully promoted this festival there for 1998 and 1999. The festival for the year 2000 will be held March 3 at the Hotel Fallsview in Ellenburg, NY. Bands already committed include **IIIrd Tyme Out, Country Gentlemen, James King** and the **Stanley Brothers**.

Winterhawk

The Winterhawk Bluegrass Festival is a four-day affair in July at the Rothvoss Farm in Ancramdale, NY. The Dry Branch Fire Squad acts as host band and this festival's popularity and attendance rival those of the earlier Berkshire Mountain Festival at Duanesburg. In addition to having many of the very top bands such as **Allison Krause and Union Station, Austin Lounge Lizards, Bill Keith, Doyle Lawson and Quicksilver, Jimmy Martin, Norman and Nancy Blake, Peter Rowan, Ralph Stanley, Seldom Scene** and dozens of others, they also offer a Thursday night band contest with cash prizes. There are five entertainment stages including a children's stage with concerts, story tellers and magicians, a teen program, workshops, instrument makers and repairmen, square dances, crafts and other vendors. The festival started in 1983, making it one of the older festivals in New York State. The 1999 festival will be the 17th annual.

Wrench Wranch Wroundup

It should be understood that the Wrench Wranch Festival is not a Penny festival even though there are some similarities. The same site is used, the same sound man, Gale Peabody, and sound system is utilized and many of the same bands play at both festivals. However, the Wrench Wranch Wroundup is exclusively a Ted Wrench production. He and his wife Brenda do all the promoting, advertising, band hiring and other pre-festival preparation. The festival is regularly held Labor Day Weekend in September, although some of the earlier ones were held after Labor Day.

In fact, the first festival was held September 15, 1984. It was a one-day get-together with sponsorship divided among Ted, Charlie Brown and Penny. The admission price was a $2.00 donation at the gate. The following year Ted took over sole sponsorship of the festival, extending it to two days, Saturday and Sunday. By 1988 the festival was a three-day weekend affair with many campers staying over until Monday.

The Wrench Wranch Wroundup festival has been the site of many humorous happenings including performances by Sweet Things, mock weddings, election of Snip City mayor and oversize bonfires by the Paps Grant crew. The bands which played at the 1998 festival included **Blue Ridge Mountain Boys, Bluegrass Melody, Cedar Ridge, Charlie Sherman and the Ridgerunners, Classic Country, Morgan String Band, Plexigrass, Smokey Greene, Stateline, Stoney Mountain** and **Wrench's Wranglers.**

Penny Memorial Day Weekend Festival

After the Afton Festival Penny was a bit gun shy about promoting festivals. However that was about to change in the Spring of 1983. On March 20 of that year Ted Wrench invited the members of Penny to visit his lumber mill in Coventryville, NY for a maple sugar party. Those invited were to bring sausage and eggs with them and Ted would provide all the pancakes and homemade maple syrup you could eat. Of course those who played an instrument brought it along and there was much picking along with the socializing.

But it was cold! Someone decided it would be better to have a party when it was a bit warmer and Memorial Day weekend was chosen as the date for that party. As far as bands for entertainment, there were only a few of the Penny members and the **Happy Hollow Boys,** with Ted Wrench on fiddle, Bob Dougherty on guitar, Claude Sherwood on bass and Chris Bubney on dobro.

Neither this party nor the one held the following year could really be called a festival. The sugaring party was held in the garage near the highway. The Memorial Weekend party was held in the field half way back to the location of the present day Wrench Wranch festivals. The second year of this festival, 1984, was actually Penny's first year as sponsor, since Ted Wrench had sponsored the first one. This year saw much more stage music. In addition to several Penny member bands other bands included the **Booze Brothers, Charlie Brown and Co., Del-Se-Nango Fiddlers, High Street Boys, The Laing Brothers, Lubeck Family Band** and **Stateline**. This was a one-day festival with a $2 admission.

For the following year, Penny's second annual festival was held at its present site out back where Ted had just finished building the pole barn. This pole barn would have additions of a kitchen, dance floor and stage throughout the coming years. The second annual Penny fest was held May 24-26 and the admission was $6.00 for the weekend. For the next thirteen years until 1998 the festival has been held on Memorial Day weekend with campers arriving on Wednesday and some staying through to Monday. The price per weekend has remained within reason, $20.00 per weekend at present with free camping in the rough and free dumping at the facility on the grounds. During the past thirteen years attendance has increased steadily to about 750 people for the 1998 festival.

One of the highlights over those years was the stage incident in 1985 when Al Eddy, bass player for **The Booze Brothers**, was aided on stage by twelve extra stand up basses. Another highlight was the initial appearance in 1989 of **Sweet Things** with four Penny members in drag. And in 1990 two bands came to the festival as campers and ended up playing on stage. These two bands were **Rose City** from Connecticut and the newly formed **Fox Family** from Old Forge, NY.

Bands which have played at the Memorial Day Weekend Fest included **Backporch Majority, Billie and The Boys, Blades of Grass, Booze Brothers, Classic Country, Cold Spring, Copper Creek, Counterfeit Bluegrass, Dark Hollow, Delaney Brothers, Diamondback Rattlers, Duke Wilson, East Windsor Git Down Bluegrass, Family of Friends, Fish 'n' Friends, Gospel Travelers, Gulf Summit Express, Happy Hollow Boys, High Street Boys, Ithaca Bluegrass, Laing Brothers, Montrose Express, Roots of Bluegrass, Smoot Family, Sochell Security, Tamarack, Twin Rivers,** and **Wholewheat Bonanza**. Bands which have played for that weekend through the years and also performed at the most recent festival in 1998 are **Blue Ridge Mountain Boys, Bluegrass Melody, Dyer Switch, Morgan String Band, Plexigrass, Spare Parts, Stateline, Stoney Mt. Bluegrass** and **Wrench's Wranglers**.

Penny Midwinter Festival

In order to raise money for a worthy cause, the members of Penny decided to hold a midwinter festival at the Deposit Fire Hall in 1985. Only Penny member bands performed and the admission charged was $2.00 at the door. The attendance was good enough for the organization to host another midwinter fest March 2, 1986 at the Sea Galley in Kirkwood, NY. This was followed by still another on December 7, 1986 also at the Sea Galley. This festival was actually the third but was called the second since there had been two that year. In any case the next one, the fourth, was held on March 1, 1987 again at the Sea Galley. The Fifth Midwinter Festival moved to the Eagle's Club in Endicott, NY and was held on March 4, 1988. The festival continued to be held at the Eagle's Club for the next three years until 1992.

In 1993 the Midwinter Fest was moved to the American Legion Hall on Jensen Road in Vestal, NY and has continued to be held there to the present. It was there that the Penny organization for several years collected canned food at the door to benefit CHOW. Cash donations were also made. In 1993, the money for the donation to CHOW was raised by having an ugly banjo player contest with cash contributions used for votes. Gary Harper won the contest in a landslide. The 1999 festival was held on March 6.

Country Music and Bluegrass Festival

Rick and Carol Twiss have been hosting this event at their Country Side Inn near Ft. Ann since 1986. Bands playing at this festival have included **Andy Pawlenko, Easy Country Band, Fred Pike, Sam Tidwell and The Kennebec Valley Boys, Hank and Irene Clothier, Jimmie Hamblin, Lyle Saunders and Border Ride, Rose City Bluegrass, Smokey Greene and The Boys** and **Stateline**.

Ransom Park

In the spring of 1986 Bill and Dorothy Stewart from Tioga Center, NY contacted the Penny organization. On behalf of the Ransom Park Association, they asked Penny for help in promoting a bluegrass festival at their local park. Bill and Dorothy wanted to know if Penny would provide such things as publicity, bands, emcees, ticket takers, etc. for a Ransom Park weekend bluegrass festival. The Park Association would take care of security and the kitchen while Penny would keep all gate receipts. Penny's Ransom Park Committee concluded that this would be a good opportunity to repay the bands that had played for the Memorial Day and Midwinter festivals for free. It was decided to invite these bands to play at this festival and divide any profit after expenses among them.

A one-day festival was held on July 27, 1986. The following year the festival grew to a three-day weekend affair held the third weekend in July. The Park Association built a very fine stage located opposite the kitchen area. For the next four years Penny groups and other local bands performed on this stage. The last Ransom Park fest was held July 1990. Some time after that 1990 performance but before the summer of 1991, the Ransom Park Association informed the members of Penny that internal organization problems would prevent them from hosting any more July bluegrass festivals.

Fortunately, the Penny July Festival Committee located another site a few miles from Ransom Park. The owners of L & L Campgrounds, Leroy and Corinne Frisbee were interested in hosting an annual July bluegrass festival. They would accommodate the Penny organization in much the same way as the Ransom Park Association had. The L & L Campground would have the food concession and Penny would have the gate receipts. This would not be the Frisbee's first foray into bluegrass. They had already promoted festivals at their campground for the past few years with the help of Carl Kithcart and Bob Schneider and Sandy Foley. For the L & L Festival, Penny grew bolder in the selection of bands, featuring **IIIrd Tyme Out, Carolina Rebels, Echo Mountain,** the **Gibson Brothers** and the **Wildwood Girls** to name only a few of the bigger bands who have performed there over the past eight years. The practice of sharing the net profits with the local bands was continued.

Grove Park

Trudy Fagan of Elmira, NY put together several free one-day festivals at Grove Park, Elmira from 1988 to 1994. The sponsors were Elmira Rug, Fagan Engineers and the Pepsi Company. The 1991 festival featured three bands, the nationally known **Bluegrass Cardinals, Summit** and local group **Plexigrass.** Trudy made a guest appearance that year playing fiddle for **Plexigrass.** In 1994 the festival featured three local bands, **Pasture Prime, Fish 'n' Friends** and Trudy's own band, **Tall Grass** with Trudy on fiddle and Gene Phillips on banjo.

Fox Family Festival

The Fox family hosts the bluegrass festival held in Old Forge each year in August since 1990. The sponsors are Al Worthan and his Mountain Music Shop and the Central Adirondack Association. The lineup each year features a balance of out-of-state bands as well as very good ones from the area including the host band **Fox Family**.

Bill Knowlton and Nick Barr were emcees at the 1998 festival which included **2nd Edition, Burnt Toast, Delaney Brothers, Gibson Brothers,** and **James King.** Dick DeNeve was at the festival with a number of his hand-crafted mandolins and dobros taking orders from those who understand that there is a waiting list for completion and delivery.

St. Lawrence Valley Bluegrass Festival

Bobbe Erdman is the promoter for this very successful festival held each year at Governeur, NY. The sponsor for the first year's festival in 1990 was The Ronald McDonald House. Sponsor for the second and third years was the E.J. Noble Hospital Auxiliary. The Governeur Chamber of Commerce sponsored the fourth, fifth and sixth years. From 1996 to the present the sponsor has been the St. Lawrence Building Fund.

The festival is held the third weekend in August at the St. Lawrence County Fairgrounds and features the talented Mike O'Reilly as emcee. The sound is provided by Gale Peabody.

Local bands featured at this festival have included the **Andy Pawlenko, Case Brothers, Craig Parsons and The Blue Ridge Mountain Boys, Dempsey Station, Gibson Brothers, Lykens Valley Boys, Plexigrass, Rosewood, Smokey Greene** and **Spare Parts**. There have also been a number of very good bands from Canada along with name bands from south of the Mason-Dixon Line.

Old Time Fiddler's Gathering at Watkins Glen

The Old Time Fiddler's Gathering is sponsored by the Arts of The Southern Finger Lakes and is held the second or third Sunday in June at the Watkins Glen New York State Park recreation hall. Over the past few years they have featured **The Delaney Brothers, Fiddlers of the Genesee, Hilton and Stella Kelly, John Kirk and Trish Miller, Mark Hamilton, Pat Kane's Little Big Band, Real Country** and **The Weir Family**. Held since 1990, the 1999 gathering will be the tenth annual. Peter Vorhees is the organizer.

Bluegrass on the Green

Ray and John Delaney and Steve Lundberg have presented a free one-day festival at Homer, NY in June from 1991 to the present. The festival regularly features two very good local bands and has included **Andy Pawlenko, Cornerstone, Delaney Brothers, Lonesome Road Ramblers**, and **Plexigrass**. The show is sponsored by radio station WXHC Homer, NY, the Homer Volunteer Fire Department, Key Bank of Homer and local merchants.

L & L Campground

Leroy and Corinne Frisbee have hosted festivals at their campground in Nichols, NY since 1991. During that time they have had several co-sponsors. In 1991 the Kithcart family helped them promote their first festival. In 1993 and 1994 Bob Schneider and Sandy Foley were co-sponsors. In 1995 Leroy and Corinne produced the festival themselves. Beginning in 1996 and up to the present they enlisted the help of the Penny organization which works closely with the Frisbees to present the L & L Campground

Festival now held each year the third weekend in July.

Bands at this festival have included **IIIrd Time Out, Carolina Rebels, Gibson Brothers, Jim & Jesse, the Stevens Family** and **The Wildwood Girls**. Local bands have included **Blue Ridge Mountain Boys, Bluegrass Melody, Cedar Ridge, Classic Country** with Ken Silvernail on guitar, Clint Lainhart on banjo, Randy Dimick on bass, Lisa Dimick on vocals, Earl Wakeman on dobro and Ralph Severcool on guitar, **Delaney Brothers, Dyer Switch, Fish 'n' Friends, Morgan String Band**, with Chris Brown on mandolin, Dave Carey on guitar, Steve DiRancho on banjo and Mark Carey on bass, **Plexigrass, Spare Parts, Stateline** and **Wrench's Wranglers**. They also held several best band contests won by **Twin Summits** and another time by **Fish 'n' Friends**.

Nanticoke Hills

Doug Ellis and Dale Jordan organized this one time only festival at Nanticoke Hills in Maine, NY in May 1991. The bands that played there included **Back Porch Majority, Delaney Brothers, Gulf Summit Express, Plexigrass, Redwood Hill** and **Spare Parts**. Gale Peabody provided the sound. Poor attendance was one of the reasons for discontinuing this festival.

Thousand Islands Bluegrass Festival

This festival is held in June each year in Clayton, NY at Captain Clayton's Campground. The festival started in 1991 and the one for 1999 will be the 9th annual. Prior to 1999, the festival promoters featured a balanced mix of major bands and local bands. Major bands have included **Bluegrass Thoroughbreds**, the **Gibson Brothers, Stevens Family**, and **Warrior River Boys**. Local bands have included **Creek Bend, Dyer Switch** and **Grass Creek**, a band from Canada. The 1999 festival will feature only **Mac Wiseman** as the headliner along with several local bands.

Corinth

In 1992 Roger Sitts held the first of his seven annual festivals in Corinth, NY. For that first festival the host band was **Smokey Greene and The Green Mountain Boys**. Interestingly enough, Corinth had been the site of the 1972 and 1973 Smokey Greene festivals. Other bands performing at the 1992 festival included **Al & Kathy Bain, Andy Pawlenko, Bear Acker and Billings Gap, Bill Matteson and B Flat Band, Cedar Ridge, Hank & Irene, Jimmie Hamblin, Fred Pike, Sam Tidwell and The Kennebec Valley Boys** and **White Mt .Bluegrass**.

Bands scheduled to play at the 1999 8th annual, Corinth Festival include **Al and Kathy Bain, Appalachian Grass, Bear Bridge** from Massachusetts, **Blistered Fingers** from Maine, **Cedar Ridge, Hank and Irene, Hill Town Ramblers, Northern Blend , Plexigrass, Redwood Hill, Shady Creek, Smokey Greene, Stateline** and **Yodeling Slim Clark**.

Lazy River

Bernie and Marlene Carney became interested in bluegrass music in 1989 when a friend gave them a bluegrass tape. "We loved it," said Marlene. They observed carefully and gleaned information about running a festival from Penny and other festival promoters. They made arrangements with the owners of the Lazy River Campground, hired the bands they wanted and held their first festival at Lazy River, Gardiner, NY in 1992.

Some of the bigger name bands playing at the Lazy River Festivals included **Bob Paisley, Boys from Indiana, Carolina Rebels, Del McCoury Band**, the

Gibson Brothers, The **Larry Stephenson Band**, The **Lewis Family**, **Paul Adkins**, **Reno Brothers**, and **Wildwood Girls**. Local bands featured at these festivals included **Burnt Hills Bluegrass Band**, **Cedar Ridge**, **Dyer Switch**, **Fish 'n' Friends**, **Smokey Greene** and **Spare Parts**. The **Gibson Brothers** were featured at all six of their festivals.

The Carneys held festivals at Lazy River for five years and then moved it to the New Paltz Fairgrounds in 1997. Growing costs for the festival site and uncertainty about a definite festival date kept them from having a summer outdoor festival in 1998. They have, however, hosted three festivals at the Granit Hotel in Kerhonkson, NY, the latest one March 27-29, 1998.

Roxbury Arts Community Center

October 9, 1994 marked the dedication of the newly renovated Community Center in Roxbury, NY in honor of Hilton and Stella Kelly. The one-day event, Fiddlers I, showcased Canadian national champion fiddlers Gerry Robichaud and Edmond Boudreau, Jay and

Molly Unger, special guest Scotsman Aly Bain and the honorees Hilton and Stella Kelly and their band the **Sidekicks**. Local teen fiddlers Laura Cortright and Sara Milonovich played "Snowflake Breakdown." Then Laura played "Golden Slippers" with Hilt Kelly, each bowing the other's fiddle.

Almost exactly one year later Fiddlers II was held at the same location. Canada was once again represented by Joe Cormier and Edmond Boudreau playing Canadian folk music. Laura Cortright and Sara Milonovich played contemporary bluegrass and folk tunes. They were followed by Earl White on fiddle, Mike Fleck on electric clawhammer banjo and Gil Sayre on guitar. **Hilton and Stella Kelly and the Sidekicks** were next, playing folk and country music. After intermission Jay and Molly Unger played some of their original compositions including "Ashokan Farewell" and a contra dance. The last performance of the day featured **Beau Thomas** from Louisiana doing Cajun tunes, backed up by local guitar player, Brian O'Connell. Since then there have been a number of one-day stringed musical programs at the Roxbury Arts Center.

Steamburg SOTC&BA

In August 1994 the Stateline Old Time Country and Bluegrass Association held their first festival. Dick and Betty Young helped to organize this festival which featured all local bands. The 1999 festival will be a one-day combination festival-flea market event.

Newark Valley

Sandie Downs is the organizer for the Newark Valley Festival sponsored by the Newark Valley Chamber of Commerce. This festival is held in June and the 1999 festival will be the third annual. Local bands playing at this festival have included **The Attic String Boys, Cedar Ridge, Fish 'n' Friends, Plexigrass, Roots of Bluegrass** and **Stateline**.

Big Apple Bluegrass Festival

This festival is held at the Baggot Inn in Riverdale, NY in November. The 1998 festival featured **Bill Keith, Burnt Toast, The James King Band, John Herald, Tony Trischka & Skyline** and **Vassar Clements**. The Sunday fiddler's convention featured Vassar Clements, Tony DeMarco, Kenny Kosek and Jeff Wisor. There was also a banjo workshop presented by Bill Keith. Tom Hanway is the organizer.

Pickin' In The Pasture

Andy Alexander's first bluegrass festival was held in Lodi, NY. in the summer of 1998. The site of the festival is actually his own sheep farm acreage. A few years ago Andy was talking with Dick Smith's brother Bill who was trying to steer Andy's banjo picking away from Trischka style toward Reno. As he looked over Andy's farm he said, "This would be a good place to hold a festival."

Having worked as a staff member at Winterhawk for the previous ten years Andy had a good background for planning a successful festival. And that is exactly what he did. He planned carefully and well, advertised widely, hired excellent bands, trained a well-coordinated staff and was fortunate enough to have good weather for the weekend.

Among those in the audience were 69-year-old George Edwards and his 93-year-old father, Dewey. From Wellsboro, PA the two were very familiar with the Canyon Country Festival held only a few miles from their farm. They drove up to the Lodi Festival particularly to see and hear Ralph Stanley, their favorite bluegrass entertainer. Dewey reminisced about his childhood, the jobs he'd held and his interest in bluegrass music. A particularly interesting fact was that as a youngster he attended grade school with Art Wooten, one of Bill Monroe's first fiddle players.

Dewey Edwards, Carl Stump and George Edwards

Bands playing during the weekend included **Adam Dewey and Crazy Creek, Bob Paisley & Southern Grass, David Hampton Band, The Delaney Brothers, Homestead, Ketch and Kritter, Mac Benford, Morgan String Band, Noah's Archistra, Ralph Stanley & the Clinch Mountain Boys, Rosewood, Stateline, Stump Hollow, Walt Koken** and the host band, **Pasture Prime.**

CNYBA Festival

The Central New York Bluegrass Association will host their first CNYBA festival at Lafayette, NY the first weekend in August 1999. The event is aided by a grant from the area Council of the Arts. Scheduled bands include **Andy Pawlenko, Delaney Brothers, Grass Creek, Haldimand County Line** from Canada, **Homestead, Lonesome Road Ramblers, Lost Wages** from Vermont, **One Song, Pasture Prime, Smokey Greene, Stump Hollow** and **Tired Hands String Band**. Ed Campbell is the 1999 festival chairperson.

Arcade Bluegrass Festival

This is a three-day festival held at Mockingbird Park in Arcade, NY. Walt Madison is the organizer.

Earl's Drive In

Earl Northrup holds several one-day fests at Earl's Drive In in Chaffee, NY.

Northeastern Pennsylvania Festivals

Windgap Festivals

The first festivals held by the Appalachian Fiddle and Bluegrass Association were in Cline's Grove, PA from 1974 to 1979. In 1979 the AF&BA bought Mt. View Park in Windgap, PA to use as a festival site. Festivals were held there by the AF&BA in August 1980 and 1981. Beset by financial difficulties and concerned about an inadequate turnout at the gate for the 1982 festival the organization's festival committee asked Harry Grant for his assistance. At that point Harry became the co-sponsor of the 1982 festival. The following year he took over the running of the festival himself and moved the date to the second weekend in June where it has remained to the present. Bands featured at Harry's festival included **Smokey Greene, Fox Family, Fred Hines and Company, Stained Grass Window, Gibson Brothers, Chubby Wise** and **Raymond Fairchild**.

In 1989 or 1990 with a secure financial base the AFBA once again became interested in having a festival of their own. In 1990 a one-day festival was held in August. In a year or two the one day festival had grown to two and then three days. At the present time the AFBA holds a three day festival in August each year.

Bands playing at the AF&BA festivals included **Smokey Greene, Stained Glass Window** and **Craig Parsons and the Blue Ridge Mountain Boys**. Performing with a band of teenagers at the 1998 festival was Paul Rowlands from Tunkhannock, PA.

Old Mill Village

The Old Mill Village is located a few miles south of New Milford, PA. The grounds are administered by the Pennsylvania Historical and Museum Commission and much of the village is not music oriented. However, in the latter part of August each year since 1976, the association has hosted, with Ben Stone as the manager, an old time and country music contest. Categories include fiddle, banjo, guitar, vocal, best band, miscellaneous and junior, under 16, and senior, over 65.

Over the years the bands playing there have included **Ed Flynn and Friends, Lockwood Mountain Boys, Real Country, Roots of Bluegrass, Spare Parts, Tamarack** and the **White Family Band**. Individuals placing in contests have included Francis Botts, Laura Cortright, Dave Denny, Larry Downey, Elwin Fiske Anthony Hannigan Steve Jacobi and Charlie MacDowell on fiddle. Jim Benson, Joann Errigo, Beverly Fiske, Doug Trotter and Duke Wilson placed in the vocal competition.

Covered bridge at Old Mill Village

In the miscellaneous category Charlie Kutney and Rudy Perkins on mandolin, Charlene Meyers and Donna Missigman on autoharp , Lisa Rich on hammer dulcimer were place winners. Dave Cavage, Carl Kithcart, Bob Lindsey, Ken Oakley, Gene Phillips, Gil Siegers and Danny White placed in the banjo competition. Bill Askew, Ed Flynn, Craig Gehrig, Gary Reynolds and Bob Zaidman placed in the guitar competition. Winners in the junior category have included Laura Cortright, Michael Cortright, Paul Rowlands, Anthony Sevilla and Sara White.

Friendship Ride

The Friendship Ride Bluegrass Festival was one of the earlier bluegrass festivals in the Southern Tier area. Gene Raymond hosted the first one at Lake Arrowhead, Little Meadows, PA in the summer of 1981. This festival was organized to promote bluegrass music and all proceeds went to the Muscular Dystrophy Association.

The second annual festival was held in May 1982 and featured the **Lockwood Mountain Boys, Penny, Roots of Bluegrass** and **North Fork Alliance**. The third and last festival was held in September 1983 and the featured bands were **Bluegrass Express, Diamondback Rattlers, Happy Hollow Boys, Lost Ramblers, Louie Setzer and the Appalachian Mountain Boys, Spare Parts, Stateline** with Brian Miller and Gene Raymond and **Two Rivers String Band** with Gil and Cathy Loveland.

Northeastern Pennsylvania Bluegrass Association

Jim Hannigan has promoted six bluegrass festivals with the help of Ron Penska. The first two were held at DiLeos in Mill City, PA in 1988 and 1989. The third event was held at the Lithia Valley Court Club in Factoryville, PA in 1990. Two more were held at the Firemen's Park in Fleetville, PA in 1991 and 1992. After a two-year hiatus, the final festival was held at Ransom, PA in 1995. All these festivals were praised for providing excellent bluegrass music at an affordable admission price.

In addition to Jim's band, **The Roots of Bluegrass**, other bands performing at these festivals included **99 Years, Back Mountain String Band, Back Porch Majority, Bluegrass Foure, Fish 'n' Friends, Fred Hines and Friends, Gulf Summit Express, Jack Sandbower and No Leeway, Louie Setzer and Friends, Lloyd Hampton and the Bluegrass Mountain Boys, Lost Ramblers, Mike Dillard and New Wings of Bluegrass, Niagara County Ramblers, Plain and Fancy, Plexigrass, Rose City Bluegrass, Spare Parts, Stained Glass Window, T. Diggins Bluegrass Band** and **Yarrow**.

Canyon Country

The Canyon Country Bluegrass Festivals are held the second weekend in July in Wellsboro, PA located in a valley between soaring peaks of the Endless Mountains. The first festival was in 1990 and the tenth annual will be held in 1999.

Over the years this festival has featured memorable bands such as **Bill Keith**, **The Rice Brothers**, **Tony Trischka** and the **Reno Brothers**. Area bands performing there have included **Burnt Toast**, **Cornerstone**, **Corning Grass Works**, **Diamondback Rattlers**, **North Fork Alliance**, **Plexigrass** and **Stained Grass Window**. The promoter is Debra Rubin.

Beach Lake

Beach Lake has been the site of the one-day indoor Steve Jacobi Fiddler's Convention since the first one in 1992. This is an informal and relaxed get-together with a sign up sheet for any performer who wishes to play a few numbers on stage. Performances are not restricted to fiddlers. Any bluegrass, old timey or string band is welcome. Over the years there have been such fiddlers as Larry Downey, Elmer Fiske, Hilton Kelly, Mark Hamilton, Harold Linkroum, Steve Jacobi's band, **Fiddlin' Around** and Steve and his wife Jennifer performing as a duo.

To celebrate the 20th anniversary of the Old Time Fiddlers, Steve and the Wayne County Fiddler's Association will combine the Beach Lake Fest with a workshop format to become the Autumn Leaves Traditional Music and Dance Festival, to be held October 8-10, 1999 at the Cherry Ridge Campground, Honesdale, PA. The weekend will consist of hands-on instructional workshops with subjects to include beginning, intermediate and advanced Irish fiddle, bluegrass and old time fiddle, banjo, guitar, flute, penny whistle, step dance, Appalachian clogging and contra dancing. In addition, there will be a community dance, several concerts, storytelling and an open mike fiddle segment. For students up to grade 12 from Wayne, Pike and Monroe Counties, all workshops will be free.

Diehl's Farmers Market Festival

Walt Laubach Sr. hosted this Jerseytown, PA festival from 1993 to 1998. Over the six years of the festival Walt featured such well known bands as **Lost and Found, Jim & Jesse, Jimmy Martin** and **The Stevens Family** as well as area bands including **Craig Parsons and the Blue Ridge Mountain Boys, Fish 'n' Friends, Fred Hines, Lloyd Hampton, Louie Setzer, Lykens**

Valley Bluegrass Boys, and **Roots of Bluegrass** with Jim Hannigan. Walt cited mounting costs as the reason for discontinuing this festival.

Fireball Bluegrass Festival

With the LeRaysville Fire Department as a co-sponsor, Gene Raymond again became a festival promoter at the LeRaysville Fairgrounds in LeRaysville, PA in June 1993. The bands for that year included host band **Family of Friends**, Gene Raymond on guitar, Andy Alexander on banjo, Susan Dow on bass and Joan Knowlton on mandolin, the **Bluegrass Dinosaurs** with Don Cooke on mandolin, Steve Belcher on bass, Mark Orshaw on guitar, Bob Schneider on banjo and dobro and Jeff Wisor on fiddle, **North Fork Alliance, Plexigrass, Roots of Bluegrass** and **Tamarack** with Gary Reynolds on guitar and Joann Errigo on bass.

1999 marks this festival's seventh year. Other local bands performing at the festival included **Blue Ridge Mountain Boys, Bluegrass Melody, Burnt Toast, Classic Country, Delaney Brothers, Dreadnought, Dyer Switch, Endless Mountain Bluegrass, Fish 'n' Friends, Moss Hill, Pasture Prime, Plexigrass, Southern Rail, Stateline, Tallgrass** and **Wrench's Wranglers**. For the past several years those in attendance have been treated to a round and square dance on Friday night. On another occasion there was a town-wide yard sale to coincide with the festival. For many years Gale Peabody has provided sound for the festival.

Merryall & Meshoppen

Bob Schneider and Sandy Foley had already co-sponsored two festivals in New York State at the L & L Campgrounds in 1993 and 1994. They promoted their own 1995 festival at Merryall, PA. The featured bands included

Burnt Toast, Cornerstone, Dreadnaught with Stevie Walker, Grass Act, Duke Wilson and Boone Trail from North Carolina, Plexigrass, along with some name bands Del McCoury, Gillis Brothers and Traditional Grass. The 1996 Meshoppen Festival bands included The Case Brothers, the Osborne Brothers, Wilma Lee Cooper and the Wildwood Girls with local bands Border City Bluegrass, Dyer Switch, Fish 'n' Friends, Plexigrass, Redwood Hill, and Stained Grass Window. Competition from other festivals brought about the end of this festival.

Starucca

The Starucca, PA festival started in 1995 by promoter Roger Glover, will host its fifth annual festival in July 1999. Bands playing at this smaller one-day festival in 1998 included Blue Ridge Mountain Boys, Delaney Brothers, Lonesome Road Ramblers, and Rural Delivery with Bob Parsons on guitar, Lucrezia Woodruff on guitar, Andrew Parsons on bass, Joe Bonafanti on banjo and Carl Gingher filling in on mandolin for Rudy Perkins who was recovering from an illness.

Blue Smoke and Bluegrass Festival

Ron Penska combines a tractor show with bluegrass music to promote this festival at Newfoundland, PA. The first event was held in June 1997 and was repeated in 1998. Featured bands included the Blue Ridge Mountain Boys, David Hampton Band, Fred Hines, Lloyd Hampton, Roots of Bluegrass and Stained Grass Window.

Bluegrass Biographies

There have been many people who have made significant contributions to the bluegrass music scene in New York State and northeastern Pennsylvania. The following men and women represent a cross-section of those who have made such a contribution, whether as an entertainer, dancer, promoter, teacher, writer or as just a friend of bluegrass. As a group their stories portray the growth of bluegrass over the past eighty years. For the most part, the brief biographies indicate that they were exposed to music by a father, mother, grandfather, uncle or other family member. In many cases they have, in turn, passed the music along to their children, thus continuing the legacy of the early fiddlers.

A. James Baudendistle
(b. August 5, 1925)

As a youngster Jim had listened to Wilma Lee and Stoney Cooper in the 1930s and Bill Monroe, Lester Flatt and Earl Scruggs and Reno and Smiley in the 1940s. Mac Wiseman and Stonewall Jackson were two of Jim's favorite radio performers. Through the 1960s and 1970s Jim would get together with local mandolin player Bruce Evans and another of his friends, Don Wheeler, who played a little on the banjo and fiddle. With these two Jim would try to emulate on his dobro the playing of 'Bashful Brother'

Oswald, whose style Jim admired.

In the fall of 1980 Jim and his wife Rita allowed a small group of novice bluegrass pickers to use his storage barn in Gulf Summit, NY for practice sessions and get-togethers. When the group played Jim would sit in with his Gibson-A mandolin. If another mandolin player arrived, Jim would switch to playing his dobro. He realized that a bass fiddle would be a welcome convenience, so he bought and provided a house bass for anyone's use at the picking sessions. When a bass player was not available Jim would pick up the bass and provide players with a steady beat.

Jim's dedication to the Penny organization and to bluegrass cannot be overemphasized. Every Friday night from September to May from 1980 to 1992 he and his wife Rita cleaned the picking area in the barn. They stoked the fire, a red hot roaring blaze in a homemade double barrel stove fueled by chunks of old railroad ties. They provided a guest book for signing, served refreshments, shoveled snow to make a path to the barn when needed and sponsored dozens of Penny and related bluegrass activities throughout the years.

About a half mile from the Gulf Summit barn, Jim and Rita own some acreage that includes a wooded section with a natural amphitheater. With the help of his family and a few Penny members, the land was partially cleared and a stage was built. This land became the site of numerous picnics, picking sessions and social gatherings in the 1980s. The Baudendistles did not limit attendance to just bluegrassers. Friends and neighbors were always welcome and made to feel part of the group.

For the past eight years the Friday night picking sessions have become more occasional than regular. However, a midweek phone call from only two or three pickers is all it takes for Jim to make ready a nearby empty house trailer where the sessions are now held. In 1987 Jim retired from his maintenance job at IBM to pursue his hobby of restoring old Ford cars.

The Delaney Brothers
Ray Delaney (b. April 22, 1953)
John Delaney (b. September 14, 1955)

Ray lives in Cortland, NY and works for the New York State Department Of Transportation as a supervisor. John works at the Research and Development Lab for Welch Allyn Medical Diagnostics.

Ray started playing the guitar at age fifteen. To improve his playing he took a few lessons from George Reese. His first encounters with bluegrass music were listening to Bill Knowlton's Bluegrass Ramble radio program in 1972 and attending a few bluegrass jam sessions held at the Hannibal Library.

In 1978 Ray was playing guitar and singing in clubs with a partner. When the partner left, Ray replaced him with brother John and they continued to work clubs and bars as a duo. In 1982 they added Pat Parsnow as their banjo player. Dave Cleaveland heard them play and encouraged them to do more brother tunes. They then added Jim Treat to play the bass. The band's first real festival performance was at the Wrench Wranch in the early 1980s. Their 1998 band had Ray on guitar, John on mandolin, Scott Corbett on banjo, Joe Davoli on fiddle and Ted Revutsky on bass.

Ray co-hosts a radio program with Steve Lundberg featuring bluegrass music Saturday night over WXHC Homer, NY. They started doing the show in July 1991. The sponsor for the first six years was Agway. The sponsors now are Cortland Asphalt and Cortland Picture Frame Co. The program consists of early bluegrass with Bill and Charlie Monroe, newer artists, local artists and finishes with two or three gospel numbers. Once each quarter they have a live band broadcast.

Ray, John and Steve Lundberg, also host a one-day festival, Bluegrass on the Green in the park in Homer, NY. This is a continuation of Hometown Bluegrass started seven years ago. The program usually features two bands and is free to the public. The sponsors are the radio station, Key Bank, Homer Volunteer Fire Department and local merchants. Over the years the featured bands have included **Andy Pawlenko, Bob Paisley, Cornerstone, Diamondback Rattlers, Dyer Switch, Plexigrass, Red-wood Hill** and **The Delaney Brothers**.

In addition to playing for their own Bluegrass on the Green festival, the Delaneys have performed at Peaceful Valley, Otisco Lake, Bainbridge Town Hall Opry, Pickin' in the Pasture, Wrench Wranch, Herkimer, Bluegrass Ramble, Fox Family and St. Lawrence Bluegrass Festival to name a few. The brothers' biggest thrill was having Bill Monroe play and sing with their band as they performed at the Three Rivers Inn in Phoenix, NY.

Ray says that bluegrass music is true to its roots, relies on content, is acoustic and started with Bill Monroe in the 1940s.

Larry Downey
(b. August 3, 1910)

Larry has worked at the EJ Tannery, as a cab driver and dispatcher and most recently as a Town of Union truck driver and highway foreman. He currently resides in Johnson City, NY.

Larry probably would not consider himself a bluegrass fiddler but he is a fiddle player who has touched the lives of dozens of bluegrassers in the area whether as a contest competitor, teacher, entertainer, picking session participant or music good will ambassador. When Gil Siegers wanted to give one of his banjo classes an idea of what bluegrass music sounded like he asked Larry to be the fiddler in a trio which included Bob Lindsey on banjo and Gene Phillips on guitar.

As a child in Westfield, PA Larry listened to the music produced on his grandfather Perry's old record player, the Edison Phonograph with its big Morning Glory Horn. The records were of the old cylinder variety and contained many of the old time fiddle tunes such as "Redwing," "Silver Bell" and "Snow Deer." These tunes stuck in his mind and later came easily to his fingers as he learned the art of fiddling.

When Larry was about seven a salesman came to the house on Rogers Avenue in Endicott and offered forty-eight fiddle lessons from DeGraff School of Music at seventy-five cents each. The offer included the fiddle upon completion of the course. Larry took the course and received the promised fiddle following the last lesson. Sometime later he was walking home after playing at a church service one winter night and slipped on the ice. That was the end of the fiddle. His next fiddle was one that the neighbor broke and threw out in the trash. He has never been without one since.

Larry played in a band called the **Tune Twisters** for Bob Grover. They played at Grover's Barn on Day Hollow Road. He played for a time in a group with Paul and Gene Roman. He has also played over several radio stations and in such music parks in Pennsylvania as Rainbow, Hibernia and Lenape. On July 4, 1964 Larry met Jehile Kirfkhuff for the first time. He recalled countless times spent playing second fiddle with Jehile and was quick to praise him as a uniquely talented fiddle player. From Jehile he learned a number of old fiddle tunes such as "Whistling Rufus," "Walking Uptown," "Bummer's Reel," "Clementine's Barrel" and "Red Haired Boy."

Over his more than 80 years of playing, Larry has owned many fiddles. A few years ago he sold an Arthur W. Howe violin which was made and given to him by that gentleman. He's a bit sorry he let it go now, but reflects that one can keep and regularly play only a few instruments. At the present time Larry owns five or six fiddles. He says that the best two were those made by Earl Wakeman of Hillcrest, NY. Larry once owned a viola that Earl wanted. He finally coerced Earl into making a five string fiddle (extra string low C) for him in exchange for the viola.

Larry's favorite tunes are "Redwing," "Snow Deer," "Barndance," "Hiawatha" (a Jehile favorite) and "Denver Belle" by Jay Unger. He's also written several fiddle tunes himself including one called "Marjorie's Reel" in B flat for his wife.

Larry talked about several fiddlers he's enjoyed playing with over the years including Todd Snover, Gil Loveland, Steve Jacobi, Hilton Kelly, Earl Wakeman and the brothers Harold and Willard Linkroum. Over the years Larry has won several important fiddle contests including the one at Osceola, NY. He still performs on stage at fiddler's gatherings, the most recent at Beach Lake, PA in the fall of 1998. He still gives lessons to a few students.

Larry Downey

Kim Fox
(b. March 19, 1966)

Kim, originally from Old Forge, NY now lives in Nashville, TN. She is the eldest of the family members in the Fox Family Band. Brother Joel, banjo player, is 32. He has a BA from Clarkson and an MA from Johns Hopkins. Sister Barb, bass player, is 28 and has an Associate Degree from Morrisville. Kim, along with all her musical success, also has received a BA degree from Potsdam.

Kim Fox

Other band members have included Mike Sharp on dobro, Kevin Church on bass, Norman Wright on mandolin and Ron Feinberg on fiddle. Both Kevin and Norman performed with **The Country Gentlemen**. On the CD *Follow My Lead*, the **Fox Family Band** has guest appearances by Doug Bartlett, mandolin, David Giegerich on dobro and Buddy Merriam on mandolin. On this particular CD Kim wrote eight of thirteen entries, including the title song.

Kim was instrumental in getting the sponsors for the Fox Family Festival, the Central Adirondack Association and Mountain Music, a stringed instrument store owned by Al Worthan. The Fox Festival started in 1990 and the 1999 festival will be the tenth annual. The Fox Family neither receives pay for performing at their festival nor do they share in any profits from the gate.

Kim and the band have performed with the **Lewis Family** at New York City's famed Eagle Tavern, at the Peaceful Valley Festival in Shinhopple, NY and have appeared on Bill Knowlton's *Bluegrass Ramble* radio show. The band also won the Winterhawk 'Best Upcoming Bluegrass Band' contest in 1989.

Of the more than forty songs Kim has written eight appear on their first album, eleven on the second. She has completed five more for the upcoming third album. At the present time Kim is living her life's dream, that of being a professional songwriter. As of the summer 1998 Kim was on her way to Nashville where she will work with Larry Cordle, an established songwriting force in that city.

Kim says bluegrass is atmosphere, improvisation, parking lot picking, a history and is the jazz of country music. She adds that bluegrass has Irish and Black roots.

Ray 'Whitey' Fritz
(January 26, 1928 – July 23, 1998)

During winter of 1980-81, the Penny Bluegrass organization was in its infancy. In fact, the name had not yet been chosen. The Friday night get-togethers consisted primarily of a bunch of beginners learning to pick together, sharing information about bluegrass and in general having the exciting experience of creating a happening.

One Friday night in December or January that

winter, Ray showed up at Jim Baudendistle's barn. Besides being very proficient at playing his Ode 5-string banjo, Ray was a very capable singer and could accompany himself credibly on his D-35 Martin. Ray was the first person to play clawhammer banjo at the barn. Furthermore, he had been attending summer bluegrass festivals for a number of years and told interesting stories in his engaging West Virginia drawl.

Ray was a faithful attendee at the barn for the rest of his life. He would often play his favorite banjo instrumental, "Clinch Mountain Backstep," or sing his favorite song, "White Dove", both Stanley Brothers tunes. Ray continually amazed the Barn pickers with his wealth of bluegrass knowledge. He seemed to know the words to every bluegrass song ever written. He later confessed that although he had not been a good student in school, he had the gift of almost total recall for printed material.

Ray Fritz

Ray had become interested in music when he was about 26 years old, in the middle 1950s. Ray's dad Clyde played clawhammer banjo when Ray was a little boy, but Ray didn't get interested in playing himself until his brother Russell started learning guitar chords. At that point Ray bought a guitar to keep up with his brother. Not long after acquiring the guitar he bought a five-string banjo and taught himself to play that.

Shortly after high school Ray went into construction work and soon became a drill boss in tunnel work. Because of his job, Ray and wife Jane moved from West Virginia to Liberty, NY in 1951, then to Boston in 1953 and finally to Hancock, NY in 1954. They soon found a house on Stockport Road just outside Hancock, where Jane still resides. There they raised two boys, Steve, 43, a construction worker and Donnie, 45, a computer company employee. Ray worked until about 1980 when he had a severe heart attack and took a medical retirement.

Ray started going to bluegrass festivals in the 1960s and camped out in a tent. Soon the tent would no longer suffice so he purchased an old Winnebago motor home. Much later he bought a brand new fifth wheel which would be the site of many late night pickin' sessions with friends.

Ray was camped near good friend Joe Bonafanti at the July 1992 Peaceful Valley Festival in Shinhopple, NY when he complained Saturday of not feeling well. He returned home and later that week suffered a fatal heart attack. Ray is remembered as a true friend of bluegrass.

The Gibson Brothers
Eric Gibson (b. October 23, 1970)
Leigh Gibson (b. October 11, 1971)

Eric and Leigh were born in Plattsburgh, NY. Intending to pursue a career in baseball, Eric attended Ithaca College for a year and a half. Realizing his musical ability was stronger than that in baseball, he returned to

Plattsburgh where he attend the local SUNY college. After receiving his Master's Degree in Communication and English Literature in 1993, Eric taught junior high and high school English for four years in the mid 1990s. Leigh was completing his college course work when the current band was formed. In 1994 Leigh received his BA degree, also from Plattsburgh, and completed some graduate work there in 1996. At the present time both are making music a full-time endeavor.

Eric and Leigh Gibson

Eric and Leigh grew up listening to bluegrass music on the radio. Their favorite performers were Lester Flatt and Earl Scruggs, the Stanleys and Mac Wiseman. They also watched the television show *Hee Haw*. Also stirring their interest was the fact that their parents had both a banjo and a guitar in the house. When they were respectively eleven and twelve they took lessons from Eric O'Hara at nearby Dick's Country Store, Eric, on the banjo and Leigh on the guitar,. The lessons were for a half hour a week and were taken for a year and a half. After learning a few songs they played and sang, with some hesitation at first, in church.

Their first performance other than at church was at Long Lake as a duo in 1987. In 1988 they played at Dave Nichols' Fest in Waddington, NY. Also in 1988 they played on stage at Smokey Greene's festival, accompanied by Don Perkins on the fiddle and Bobbe Erdman on bass.

Both Eric and Leigh knew Junior Barber as an employee of the college at Plattsburgh. At Christmas vacation time during the winter of 1991 the three of them got together for a picking session and decided to form a band. Jack McGowan from Canada, who was an acquaintance of Junior's, became the band's first bass player. When Jack began to have passport trouble getting across the border for the band's U.S. gigs, Junior's son Mike replaced him in the band. For some of the band's early performances Mike also doubled as the sound man.

The band members cut their first records in Virginia with Hay-Holler Records. At that time they made four records, three of the band and one of Junior's instrumentals. Their first album was *Long Forgotten Dream* with Doobi Shea Studios at Ferrum, VA. The second album was *Spread Your Wings*, made in Louisa, KY. Junior's instrumental, *Stone Bottom Boogie*, was recorded in Vermont. The band's latest album, *Another Night of Waiting* was cut in Nashville at Eleven O Three Studio. At the present time this album is listed in the top twenty on the *Bluegrass Unlimited* album chart. Their single "She Paints a Picture" written by Eric is listed in the top ten on the singles chart. They have recently signed with the Ricky Scaggs Recording Company's Ceili Music Division.

The Gibson Brothers band was honored recently when they were asked to play at the Ryman Auditorium for the *Bluegrass Awards Show* on April 4, 1998. A more recent accolade came when it was announced that **The Gibson Brothers** had won the "Emerging Artist of the Year" award at the 1998 IBMA awards presentations. They also received the *Bluegrass Now* Fan's Choice Award for Best Emerging Artist in 1998.

Eric and Leigh declare bluegrass to be bluesy, country roots music and it's "gotta have a 5-string in it." They both agree that bluegrass started in 1945 when Scruggs joined Lester Flatt and Bill Monroe.

Smokey Greene
(b. March 10, 1930)

Smokey's musical history provides an excellent example of bridging the gap from country and hillbilly music to bluegrass. As a youngster of sixteen he learned to play the tenor banjo and played and called square dances for **Yodelin' Slim Clark**. While playing country and square dance music he also learned to play the mandolin, fiddle and guitar. In 1947, with a brother and sister-in-law, he formed the **Greene Family Band**. In 1948 he joined the Air Force and in 1955 was stationed in California where he played guitar in a country band. As the leader of the band he found that he was supplying the members with his own cigarettes so he started buying them each a pack a night and deducted the cost from their share of the pay. As a consequence they started calling him Smokey. He took the name for his band calling it **Smokey Greene and the Greene Mountain Boys** from that time until about 1970 when he changed the name of the band to **Smokey and The Boys**.

Discharged from the Air Force in 1957 he returned East and attempted to make a living by playing music in addition to his day jobs. In 1958 he moved to Easton, NY and began to gradually build up a reputation as an entertainer in the area. By 1960 he was working a regular job six days a week and playing music as a single five nights, mostly four and five hour gigs.

In 1960 he formed a band in which he played guitar with Jimmie Hamblin on fiddle, Dan Dutra on banjo and Dick Richards on bass. At this time there were no local bluegrass festivals. However there were country parks and single day shows at schools, clubs and resorts in the area. **Smokey and the Greene Mountain Boys** were hired for these one-day affairs as the opening act for such notables as Ernest Tubb, Hank Thompson, Merle Haggard, Willie Nelson and any number of the regulars who worked the WWVA Jamboree.

By 1966 Smokey had made music his full time profession. In addition to his playing he opened a night club in Schuylerville, NY. Having attended several bluegrass festivals in Virginia, Maryland and Pennsylvania he was so enthused by the bluegrass sound that he began hiring bluegrass acts for his club. Over the next few years he found that acts such as **Reno and Smiley**, **Bill Harrell**, **Country Gentlemen**, **Don Stover** and **Charlie Moore** would double the normal attendance at his club shows.

In 1970 he moved to Glens Falls, NY where he opened a larger nightclub. He also took on the responsibility of being a disc jockey for four hours on Friday nights and more than six hours on Saturday. He would work at the radio station from 6 am Saturday until noon and then rush across town to his club to continue the broadcast live.

Smokey began having his own festivals in 1972. His first two festivals were held in Corinth, NY. The third one was in Ft. Ann in 1974. The fourth through tenth festivals were held in Saratoga through 1981. The festival was then moved to the Washington County Fairgrounds in Saratoga in 1982 where Smokey continued his festivals until 1988.

During his festival promotion years Smokey's band consisted of Brian Jaguire on mandolin, Jim Warren on dobro and Don Hudson on bass. Smokey's sons Scott and Arlin also played in the band for a number of those years. In addition to playing at his own festival the band also played throughout the Northeast as a featured attraction. In 1995 Smokey decided to call it quits as far as the band was concerned and began working as a single. In this new capacity he is still a headliner at area festivals.

Jim Hannigan
(b. December 14, 1935)

Jim works for the Commonwealth Telephone Company out of Ransom, PA. Born and raised in West Virginia Jim became interested in music at about age thirteen. As a youngster he heard his grandfather play the fiddle and banjo. He listened to a program over station WCHS Charleston, WV called *The Old Farm Hour* with Bradley Kincaid playing guitar, Grandpa Jones on banjo and Clark Keitenger on fiddle.

When he was fourteen, Jim took guitar lessons from friend Charles Farren, then switched to mandolin at age sixteen. At sixteen and a half he joined the Army and while in the service played country music with other pickers. A man named Paul Woolwine played fiddle there and taught Jim the basics. He served in both Korea and Germany. He left the service in 1958 and went to work for Bell Telephone in West Virginia.

In 1960 Jim moved to California where he played electric guitar in a swing band. In 1961 he returned to West Virginia. In 1962 he moved to Pennsylvania where he played in a band with **Louie Setzer and the Appalachian Mountain Boys** with Jim on fiddle, Louie on guitar, Fred Servant on mandolin, Shorty Newcomber on banjo and Fred Sharp on bass.

In 1971 Jim formed his own band, the **Roots of Bluegrass**, playing fiddle and mandolin along with son Anthony on mandolin and fiddle, Dave Cavage on banjo, Louie Setzer on guitar and Walt Laubach Jr. on bass. The present band consists of Jim, Bobby Nora on guitar, Steve Shellhammer on banjo and Walt Laubach on bass. **Roots**

of Bluegrass has played at many festivals in the area including Governeur, STBA, Bluegrass Ramble, Jerseytown, Wrench Wranch and Jim's own festival. They are scheduled to play at a number of 1999 festivals.

In 1988 Jim, along with Barb White and Ron Penska, formed the Northeastern Pennsylvania Bluegrass Association. The organization issued membership cards but did not have a newsletter. For eight years they hosted a picking session at Keystone College in Factoryville, PA on the first Sunday of the month from September to April. Conflicts led to the end of these sessions in 1996.

Jim was instrumental in producing six bluegrass festivals, two at Mill City, one at Factoryville, two in Fleetville and the final one in Ransom, all in Pennsylvania. Jim has also played his fiddle and mandolin for a number of commercial bluegrass tapes including those by the Lloyd Hampton and the David Hampton bands. After Jim leaves the stage at any bluegrass festival he can be found at someone's campsite participating in the field picking playing either his mandolin or fiddle. When asked to give a definition of bluegrass, Jim said, "It's a poor man's jazz."

Gary Harper
(b. November 25, 1947)

Gary works as a long-haul truck driver. He grew up around stringed music and remembers his Uncle Bob Demp playing an instrument in the house in Lisle, NY. He went to his first bluegrass festival in 1953 at Rainbow Park in Maine, NY to hear **Reno and Smiley**. In 1957, Fred Johnson and Bob Mavian visited and picked with the locals at the house with Gary's father, Harvey and his Uncle Bob.

Around 1959 or 1960 Gary knew he wanted to learn to play the banjo after he listened to "Jimmy Brown" and "Flint Hill Special" on a borrowed Flatt and Scruggs recording. His father put four strings on a guitar, tuned them as a banjo and told Gary that when he learned three songs he'd buy him a banjo. In a short time the three songs were learned and Gary was given a Montgomery Ward banjo. Around 1962 his father bought him a new Gibson Mastertone.

Gary learned to play his banjo by listening to records and watching the banjo players at stage shows. In the early 1960s he went to Echo Lake and saw **Jim and Jesse**, **Bill Harrell and the Virginians** and **Carl Story**. He soon learned to substitute metal finger picks for plastic. Once he jammed with Mac Wiseman on stage there. Virginian Don Stover was one of Gary's favorite banjo players at that time. At one of these shows Gary asked banjo player Betty Ames to show him some licks on the banjo. She refused, telling him that she had too many bad habits in her playing. Another time he asked Alan Shelton to give him some banjo tips. After Shelton finished his stage show he put Gary off, saying the sun was too hot to have his banjo out. Later when Shelton was jamming in the shade down by the lake he asked Gary if he was ready for a lesson. Angered by the earlier refusal, Gary declined Shelton's offer.

It was sometime in 1961 or 1962 that Gary saw **Wilma Lee and Stoney Cooper** at the Whitney Point Fair and heard Vic Jordan play the banjo there. He remembered seeing the **Laing Family Band** perform at Echo Lake. **The Voices of Bluegrass** with Bucky Walters and Jeff and Marlene Wisor also performed there.

In the 1960s Gary played in a band called **The Harper Family** with Harvey on the dobro, a family member Pat on bass, Gary on banjo, Ed and Bud Pierce on guitar, Bob Wilson on guitar and Jack Tryon on mandolin.

In 1962 and 1963 the **Diamond Valley Ramblers** performed in the Binghamton area with members Kit Kithcart, Kenny Marsh and Steve Walker. When Steve left to play with another band Gary was asked to join the **Ramblers**. With Kit on guitar, the band played over station WEBO Owego. They also played on Channel 12 television out of Binghamton. Gary remembers seeing Bob Wilson and Jack Tryon there. Both Jack and Bob played for the **Diamond Valley Ramblers** on various occasions.

In the late 1960s Gary was playing country music and bluegrass at the Silver Dollar in McDonough with a band called the **Corn Cobblers** consisting of Ray Brownell, Stiver Brout and Dave Denny. In 1973 they won first prize for best country group at the Syracuse Fair. In 1974 Gary was playing in **Just Another Bluegrass Band** with Charlie Kutney on guitar, Jim Ryan on mandolin, Gary on banjo and Harvey on bass. The group played on Bill Knowlton's *Bluegrass Ramble* program.

In 1975 Gary played his banjo part time with a group from Madison County called the **Margaret Sanger Rhythm Boys** organized by Geoff Noyes. Other members of the band were Jim Allen on mandolin, Bill Day on guitar, Ley Pietroski on guitar and Gene Czajowski on bass. Gary says that because Margaret Sanger was a well-known advocate of birth control, they did not get many good playing jobs and Goeff changed the name of the band to **Seneca Turnpike**.

In 1977 Gary met Barney French and formed a band with Barney on guitar, Gary on dobro and Joe Ganna on harp. They played country music in bars, occasionally getting an opportunity to play a little bluegrass music. When the band members met Al Eddy, they soon invited him to play bass in the group and the **Booze Brothers** band was formed. The band performed at bluegrass festivals for the next twelve years.

Gary also played part time in Billie Karcher's band **Billie and the Boys** in the late 1980s and through the 1990s. In 1995 and 1996 he played 5-string in the band **The Blue Ridge Mt. Boys** led by Craig Parsons on guitar with Duane Ormsby on dobro, Brad Miller on guitar, Jim Callan on bass and Ron Parsons (Craig's father) on guitar and vocals.

When asked if Bill Monroe had founded bluegrass, Gary insisted that Monroe's contribution as the father of bluegrass occurred only after Earl Scruggs joined **The Blue Grass Boys** in the fall of 1945.

Carl Hedges
(b. September 23, 1920)

Carl currently resides in Hallstead, PA. Born and raised in Missouri he got his first fiddle at the age of seven. He was taught to play the fiddle by his Great Uncle Rolla West. By the time Carl was thirteen he was playing for local dances and at age seventeen led his own band. On Saturdays the band would play old timey music and square dances at a dance hall.They also played at house dances during the week on Wednesday and Friday. Interestingly, in Missouri the square dance callers would talk rather than sing the dance calls and sometimes,the dancers would call their own squares. In addition to the fiddle, Carl also learned to play the banjo and mandolin.

While Carl was growing up in Missouri he listened to WSM Nashville, WLVA New Orleans and WWVA, Wheeling, WV. In the 1920s he listened to **The Possum Trotters, Ridge Runners, Uncle Dave Macon and the Dixie Dewdrops, Roy Acuff, The Delmores, Wilma Lee and Stoney Cooper** and **Bill Monroe and The Blue Grass Boys**. As a young man Carl performed over radio station WDAF, Kansas City.

Carl entered a fiddling contest in 1939 in Missouri and won, playing the "True Love Waltz" and "Ragtime Annie." The prize was the opportunity to go to Nashville and play four tunes on stage with Roy Acuff over WSM. Carl recalls that two of the tunes they played were "The Great Speckled Bird" and "Wabash Cannonball." While in Nashville he met Howdy Forrester who was Acuff's fiddle player at that time.

He moved East in 1969 where he practiced his profession as an electrical engineer. He and two others bought into the Singer Company which sold driver trainers and learning systems with closed circuit television. During the years he was working and raising a family with his first wife Ethel he put his fiddling aside, playing only occasionally.

In 1974 Carl met Jehile Kirkhuff at Lenape Park in Philadelphia where the two of them found that they had a good deal in common as related to music and fiddling. In 1979 Ethel died of cancer. That same year Carl joined the Del-Se-Nango Fiddlers group and soon began to play the fiddle regularly at their gatherings and jam sessions.

Carl Hedges

In March of 1981 Jehile Kirkhuff died and Carl was one of the group of thirty or forty friends who played their fiddles at Jehile's grave side, 'fiddling him to heaven.' After the ceremony, the Fireman's Auxiliary of Lauten, PA, invited all the mourners to a buffet dinner at the Fire Hall.

Carl found himself seated next to Doris Diffendorf and her sister Ginny Pompeii. The three had a nice visit during the buffet and Doris expressed an interest in old timey music. About a month later Doris called Carl to get his advice on buying a mandolin. She bought the mandolin and Carl asked her for a date. They were married a few months later on August 21, 1981.

From 1979 until only recently Carl played his fiddle regularly and performed over much of New York State and Pennsylvania at fiddle contests and Del-Se-Nango functions. For the past few years health problems have forced him to cut back on his fiddling.

Elmer Hoover
(b. April 11, 1937)

Elmer lives in Springville, PA on the farm he worked for many years. He was four or five years old when he was given a potbelly mandolin by his Uncle Bill. He recalls that many in his family were musical. Uncle Bill played the fiddle as did Elmer's great grandfather John Miles from Camptown. Elmer particularly remembers his grandfather Miles playing a tune called "Stoney Point" also known as "Wake Up Susan." His grandfather Miles was a contemporary of the well known local fiddler George Graham, who was one of Jehile Kirkhuff's teachers.

When Elmer was eight or nine he taught himself to play the guitar after only a few lessons. An early guitar player whose style Elmer favored was Clayton Delaney. Other favorites are Doc Watson, Clarence White and Tony Rice. Elmer listened to Bill Monroe sing "Mule Skinner Blues" over an old battery radio. He also heard Ernest Tubb over WSM. He listened to performances by Roy Acuff and Hank Snow over stations WWVA and WJJD. Whenever **Wilma Lee and Stoney Cooper** played in the area in the 1940s, he had the opportunity to talk to and jam with them when their stage show was concluded.

Elmer says that he "also learned to play the banjo,

first a four string, then five in 1950, both with picks. No one even knew how to tune a five string at that time. I picked up a lot of my banjo playing by listening to the radio." Back in those days there were no how to books, or even teachers. Elmer had to learn the banjo the hard way, by trial and error, listening to the radio and by trying to copy the slowed down speed of a phonograph record. Elmer says that banjoist Bill Dailey's playing had a big influence on his style.

Elmer was one the first and few in the area to play bluegrass music on the radio. "We called it early country or hillbilly back then," he says. He played on the radio in Owego, Sayre, Binghamton and Scranton. He also did some live television shows along with appearances at music parks and schools. On several occasions he performed with Kit Kithcart, Kenny Marsh, Bob Wilson and Jack Tryon.

L to R: Tom Richards, Dick Dobrosielski, Howard Weible, Ray Rinker and Elmer

When **Wilma Lee and Stoney Cooper, Buck Graves, Mac Wiseman, Reno and Smiley** or **Flatt and Scruggs** would come to the area to perform at a local music park they would often stay at Tunkhannock. There, with Elmer and a few other dedicated pickers, they would "pick all afternoon and half the night." On many occasions Elmer's band, **The Back Mountain Boys**, or one like his would be the front band to play first and warm up the crowd. At first the visiting bands played only on Saturday. Then people in attendance at music parks in places like Sayre, Hazelton, Williamsburg and Pittston would begin to stay over. Eventually this led to the two-day and three-day festivals.

One of the highlights of Elmer's bluegrass music career came in 1958 when his band **Back Mountain Boys** played for Carlton Hainey's *Old Dominion Barn Dance* at WRVA in Richmond, Virginia. The band then was composed of Elmer on banjo, Larry Brobst on vocals and guitar, Dick Dobrosielski on vocals and guitar and Tom Richards on mandolin. Other members of the band throughout the 1950s included Keith Russell (who also played with Wilma Lee and Stoney Cooper) on bass, Leon Jenkins on guitar, George Benson on steel guitar, Howdy Weibel on guitar, Ray Rinker on fiddle and Arnie StClair on bass.

Bluegrassers of today are still trying to get Elmer to show them some licks on the banjo or dobro whenever he attends a festival picking session or when they are visiting him at his home. Jim Baudendistle isn't alone when he touts Elmer as "the best banjo and dobro player around these parts."

Ferris (Kit) Kithcart
(March 19, 1927–September 22, 1965)

Kit began playing old country or bluegrass music in the Binghamton area in the 1940s. With Stuffy Rouse on mandolin, Ray Rinker on fiddle, Kenny Marsh on bass and

Kit on the 5-string, their band, **The Diamond Valley Ramblers**, became well known in the area. In addition to playing over radio stations WEBO Owego and WINR Binghamton, NY Kit performed, announced and worked as a disc jockey over WEBO.

Ferris 'Kit' Kithcart

The Diamond Valley Ramblers were often the opening act for such out-of-town main attractions as **Jim and Jesse, Reno and Smiley** and **Jimmy Martin** when they appeared at local music parks like Echo Lake and Rainbow Park. Some other musicians in the band included Gary Harper, Elmer Hoover, Jack Tryon and Bob Wilson.

In addition to passing his musical skills along to his children Carl, Rod and Terry, Kit also gave banjo and guitar lessons to area players Bucky Walters, Bob Lindsey, Roy Matthews, Jeff Wisor and Gil Laing. While as young men Jeff Wisor, Gene Johnson and Bob Mavian were attending school in the area, they were often found at Kit's home as invited guests for a jam session. Bob Mavian currently is the mandolin player for the **Case Brothers**.

At one point in his career, Kit, along with Hal Casey of Syracuse, played over station WWVA in Wheeling, WV. In addition he also worked as a disc jockey there. When Kit died of a heart attack in the fall of 1965 he left behind a legacy of reverence for bluegrass music and a career that had touched and influenced dozens of aspiring bluegrass musicians.

Bill Knowlton
(b. October 20,1938)

It's Saturday morning 10 am. The taped bluegrass music has been turned off. Hundreds of bluegrass fans are seated in front of the stage waiting for a clanging of cowbells and the appearance of the man dressed in outlandish stripes, colors and baggy pants. Wearing his well decorated straw hat, Bill Knowlton appears at a mike to one side of the stage, cowbells reverberating in his hand. Another bluegrass festival is about to get under way. Bill welcomes the crowd to the first or second or -nth annual festival, makes a few announcements, perhaps exchanges barbs with well-meaning hecklers and steps aside to allow the first band to come on stage. While the mike checks are being done and the band is getting ready to play, he mentions any awards or accolades the band has received lately or he might offer some anecdotal information about the group or some of its members. When the band is ready to play, he announces them with gusto and another ringing of the bells and then steps quietly off stage.

Thousands of bluegrass fans have witnessed this scene hundreds of times in the past twenty-six plus years. Bill's delivery is always the same, considerate, professional and with the conviction that his style and promotion of bluegrass is something of value. He has organized, promoted, videoed, filmed, emceed, written about bluegrass and in turn been written about for the last three decades. He is a walking encyclopedia of well known and arcane bluegrass facts and anecdotes which he will share with anyone at the drop of the hat. He is a charter member of the CNYBA as well as a member of a half dozen other bluegrass organizations in the state. He has met and talked to almost every known bluegrass performer in the United States and is on a first name basis with all of them. About the only thing he hasn't done is play an instrument in a band or jam session.

Bill's first foray on radio was as a panelist on a New York City program called *What's Right With Teenagers* over station WWRL. In 1959 he introduced the *Bluegrass Ramble* program over radio station WFUV in Fordham, NY, the first all bluegrass show in New York City. He finished his stint there in 1960 and moved to WBZY in Torrington, CT where he had a one hour show on Sundays. He was there until 1962.

After graduating from Fordham with a degree in Communication Arts, Bill joined the U.S. Air Force in 1962. He attended Officer Training School and spent eleven years on active duty. He then spent another seventeen years as a reservist retiring from the service in 1990 as a Lieutenant Colonel. He also held the civilian position of Public Affairs Officer for the U.S. Army Syracuse Recruiting Battalion until he retired from that in 1993.

Bill Knowlton

After his Air Force assignment to Syracuse in 1973, Bill resurrected the *Ramble* with a 9:00 to 12:00pm Sunday night show over radio stations WCNY in Syracuse, WUNY in Utica and WJNY in Watertown. From 1980 to 1985 he aired 52 half hour television shows called the *Bluegrass Ramble* for Eastern Educational Television Network. The reruns followed for 8 or 10 more years. The TV program was presented over WCNY Syracuse and was broadcast over the Northeastern United States, Texas, Alabama, Ohio and California. The shows were taped live and there were only one or two retakes.

A favorite anecdote of Bill's involves **The Country Gentlemen**. The bluegrass band had been entertaining at Captain Max's Clam Shack in Syracuse, NY in 1964. They had gone on to Montreal for a playing date and were on their way home when they stopped at the Syracuse Language Lab to make their initial recording of "Bringing Mary Home," along with 12 other songs. At that time the band consisted of Charlie Waller on guitar, John Duffy on mandolin, Eddie Adcock on banjo and Ed Ferris on bass.

Bill hosted many local bands and personalities on the Bluegrass Ramble show including **Smokey Greene, Joe Val, Tompkins County Horseflies, The Henrie Brothers, The Lockwood Mountain Boys, Moonshine Hollow, Andy Pawlenko** and **The Smokey Hollow Boys,** Freddie Bartlett and Old Lee Moore, the 'Coffee Drinking Nighthawk'.

Bill recalls one of his most memorable guests, Hal Casey, as a fine fiddler who plays modern country music along with bluegrass. Another is Granny Sweet who passed her knowledge of fiddling on to many others and who also received the Jefferson Award for her service to youth. Lee Cross is remembered as an avid bluegrass fan who always seemed to be in the front row of the studio audience and who missed few of the taping sessions.

Among all his awards and accomplishments, Bill's most cherished achievement was being named IBMA's Broadcast Personality of the Year in 1997.

The Laing Brothers
Bill Laing (b. October 7, 1934)
Gil Laing (b. September 2, 1941)

Bill lives in Bainbridge, NY. Now retired, Bill was a supervisor at At a Glance Calendar Company. Bill got his first guitar at age eight. At that time some of his family members played hillbilly and square dance music. He'd heard his great uncles, **The Calhoun Brothers** play bluegrass, that is hillbilly, music at Andes, NY when he was a youngster. While still in junior high school Bill played for school dances in a band called **The Tumbleweed Boys**. Band instruments included clarinet, accordion, coronet and guitar. He called his first square dance when he was thirteen years old.

One night when Bill was working at a second job with the police department he stopped John Hull for speeding. When he saw a banjo case in the back of the car he started talking to the man about music. John convinced Bill to take his wife, Doreen and his brother Gil and his wife Ann to Berryville, VA for their first bluegrass festival in 1967. They continued to attend that festival yearly from 1968 to 1970.

Gil lives in Earlsville, NY and is an accountant for NY Power Company. Gil recalls learning to play the guitar when he was in the third grade. After listening to a Jimmy Martin record in the early 1960s Gil ordered an RB 250 banjo from Jack Forsyth the next day. The banjo arrived at Gil's home at Christmas time 1963. When he got out of the Navy in 1964 he took banjo lessons from Kit Kithcart and Jeff Wisor.

The boys' grandfather, father, uncle and other family members all played stringed instruments, although not the banjo. Bill and Gil said there was a banjo around the house but that no one ever tried to play it.

Bill and Gil formed a duo and played in the 1958 *Telethon* in Binghamton, NY. Gil played the guitar and Bill played the mandolin. They played at Echo Lake in the

1960s as a family band backing up such acts as **Crazy Elmer** and **Jim and Jesse**. There they met Bucky Walters, Jeff and Marlene Wisor, the **Voices of Bluegrass**. In the 1970s the Laings played one-day fests throughout New York and Pennsylvania. Once, while playing at the Rondevoo in Gilboa, NY, they were heard by Bob Bacon, a D.J. from Albany, NY. He asked them to open for the performing arts show at Saratoga, NY in 1967. In the early 1980s the **Laing Family Band** played at the Town Hall Opry in Bainbridge, NY where they still currently perform.

Bill and Gil Laing

The **Laing Family Band** played Hunter Mountain in 1985, then again in 1986. They were the first bluegrass band to play at that festival. In 1986 they met another bluegrass band performing there. The band was called **The Legends of Bluegrass** and at that time was composed of Bill Monroe, Jim and Jesse, Mac Wiseman, Ralph Stanley and Alan Shelton.

The family band currently consists of Bill on guitar, Gil on banjo, Bill's sons Larry on bass and Paul on bass and guitar, Gil's son Andy on banjo and guitar and brother Dan Laing, the original bass player. Other non-family members of the band have included Doug Bartlett on fiddle and mandolin, Arnie Russell from Saugerties on fiddle, Perry Cleaveland on mandolin and Matt Arnold on fiddle.

Bill and Gil, along with wives Doreen and Ann, held their first Laing Family Bluegrass Festivals in 1982 and 1983 in Bainbridge, NY sponsored by the Chamber of Commerce. For the years 1984 to 1991 they moved to Oxford, NY where they were sponsored by the Lion's Club. Then the festival moved back to Bainbridge where they themselves took over the role of sponsorship for 1992 and 1993. For the years 1994 and 1995 they held the festival at the Norwich, NY Fair Grounds. In 1996 the festival sponsorship was assumed by Lynn and Aileen Oliver and Al and Thelma Evans. However, the **Laing Family Band** still performs there.

Clint Lainhart
(b. May 9, 1930)

Clint worked for thirty-one years in a management position. He retired from IBM in 1984 and has worked part time since. He lives in Endicott, NY.

Clint was about 5 or 6 when he first became interested in music. He listened to Bill Monroe, Ernest Tubb and Wilma Lee and Stoney Cooper over WJJD in

Chicago, WGY in Cincinnati and Nashville radio on Saturday nights. His brother taught him a few chords on the guitar. Then his sister taught him a few chords on the banjo. After becoming somewhat proficient on guitar and banjo he learned to play the fiddle, bass, accordion, jews harp and harmonica. In 1945 he played trumpet in the Vestal High School Band. In 1946 he played in a family band with brother Jerry Lainhart and sisters Hilda and Bev Gurney where they played fiddle, guitar, banjo and accordion.

From the time he played in this family group to the present, the bands he's played in and the individuals he picked with read like a Who's Who. In 1948 he played in a band called the **Rhythm Makers** with Dick Stanton on guitar and Clint on banjo. In 1950 he was with the **Sunset Rangers** with Neil Thompson on guitar, Paul Thompson on fiddle, Dick Stanton on guitar, Don Lawrence on bass and Clint on the accordion and banjo. The year 1951 saw him with **Frank Okie and the Happy Jacks** with Frank Occhiato on fiddle, Dick Stanton on guitar, Don Lawrence on bass and Clint on accordion.

In 1952 he joined the army and was stationed in Trieste, Italy. "With many different individuals we played for clubs, company parties, taught square dancing at service clubs and put on variety shows. It was in the army that I learned to play the "Orange Blossom Special" from a serviceman from Georgia," he says.

After his stint in the army Clint joined the **Rhythm Pals** with Bill Carmen on guitar, Les Crump on guitar, Don Lawrence on bass, Jerry Lainhart on doghouse, Rusty Adams as a vocalist, Clint on guitar and banjo and Gene Hawley on accordion. The **Rhythm Pals** played over local radio stations WKOP, WINR and WEBO. Rusty Adams, by the way, once played in Ernest Tubb's band and went on to form his own group which toured in England. Adams also spent some time in Nashville where he made records, did comedy and impersonations. Clint recalls playing at Hilltop Park in Waverly, NY on a Sunday afternoon in the

Clint Lainhart

1950s. Also performing that day were **Gene Shepard**, **Hawkshaw Hawkins** and **Crazy Elmer**.

In 1955 Clint was a member of the **Art Thurber Band** with Art on tenor banjo, Russ Avis playing piano and Clint on guitar and accordion. In 1956 it was the **Gene Morey and Country Pals Band** with Gene on guitar, Russ Avis on drums and Clint playing accordion. The year 1960 saw him with the **Pat Vroman Band** with Pat on guitar, Jim Miller on guitar, Frank Chess on bass and Clint on accordion.

In 1962 he played with the Danny Oakes trio also called **Danny Oakes and The Country Chords** with Danny on bass, Pete Calvasina on accordion and Clint on guitar and banjo. Other players in the band included Gene Hawley on accordion, Cactus Mike Beddoe on accordion, Phil Scarinzi on drums, Ferris Lebous on drums and Tim Farrell on fiddle. In 1979 Clint played in the **Todd Proctor Band** with Todd on guitar, Vic Morey on drums, and Clint on guitar. Also in 1979 he played with **Gene Morey and the Country Classics Band** with Gene on guitar, Marty Mancini on bass, Vic Morey and Phil Scarinzi on drums and Clint on guitar and banjo.

In 1981 Clint joined **John Woods and the Prairie Ramblers** with John on accordion, Cleo Woods on bass, Jim Conrad on guitar, Bob Forbes on fiddle, Daron Shultes on drums, Steve Woodward on drums, Gale Peabody on bass guitar and Clint on guitar and banjo. It was in 1981 that Clint became interested in bluegrass when he met Brian Miller and Gene Raymond at a Penny picking session at the Barn in Gulf Summit, NY. He soon joined the **Stateline** band with Gene Raymond on guitar, Brian Miller on bass guitar, Joe Ganna on harp, Michelle Miller on fiddle and Clint on banjo. This band played at any number of local festivals and also did a couple of performances in Ottawa, Canada. Later additions to the band included Carl Kithcart on banjo, Steve DiRancho on banjo, Tom Quigley on mandolin and Jim Pritchard on guitar.

While still playing in the **John Woods** and

Stateline bands Clint did triple duty when he joined Gene Clayton's **Spare Parts** bluegrass band with Gene on guitar, Bob Hazen on mandolin, Patty Smith on bass, Tom Richards on mandolin, Mary Richards on guitar and vocals and Clint on banjo. Other members over the years included Carol Ripic on bass, Ken Oakley on bass, Duane Ormsby on dobro and John Evanick on dobro.

In 1992 Clint joined still a fourth band first called **Gospel Travelers** then **Classic Country** with Ken Silvernail on guitar, Lisa Dimick singing vocals, Randy Dimick on bass, Earl Wakeman on violin and dobro, Ralph Severcool on guitar and Clint on banjo and guitar. At the present time Clint is still performing with the **John Woods** and **Classic Country** bands. Clint remembers jamming with Kit Kithcart, Steve Walker and Bucky Walters, when Steve and Bucky were teenagers.

Among his many accomplishments and awards the two of which he is most proud are his induction to the NY State Country Music Hall of Fame in Cortland, NY in 1990 and his winning the banjo contest at the 1995 Bloomsburg Fair in Pennsylvania. He also has fond memories of his participation in the **Sweet Things** productions he took part in including *Sweet Things, Little Things, Sing Sing Things* and the *Coventryville Hillbillies*.

Clint's definition of bluegrass music is simple, acoustic stringed instruments. He says that in his opinion bluegrass started with Monroe, Flatt and Scruggs and Reno and Smiley.

Lockwood Family
Mary Lockwood
(b. December 8, 1938)

Mary lives in Afton, NY. She was the bass player and the co-leader of **The Lockwood Mountain Boys** band along with her third eldest son, Tim. Rick, the second eldest son learned to play an old guitar of Mary's when he was a teen. He taught Tim to play the guitar and soon Tim was playing both the guitar and mandolin. Since Tim thought that the mandolin played a major role in bluegrass music, he listened closely to bluegrass records in an effort to master the mandolin player's techniques. He acquired a few instructional books and taught himself to play the banjo, fiddle and bass. He then taught brother Jeff to play the guitar.

Back Row: Tim, Jeff, Mary Sr. Front Row: Jonathan, Mary Jr, Joshua

In 1978 or 1979 the family organized the band with Tim on mandolin and fiddle, Jeff on guitar, Bob Lindsey from nearby Port Crane on banjo and cousin Kirk Lockwood on bass. Within two years Tim had taught his mother Mary to play the bass. She replaced cousin Kirk in the band. Soon it became evident that the younger members of the family were good enough to make the band a one-family enterprise. Jonathan on mandolin, Joshua on banjo and daughter Mary on mandolin were added to the band as they became proficient with their instruments and singing ability.

The band played schools, fairs, festivals, radio and television. A memorable outing was at the Opry in Bainbridge, NY, where their performance in September 1980 was the first bluegrass offering at that venue. They also performed at Labrador Mountain in Truxton, NY. Pennsylvania outings included Old Mill Village and Lake Arrowhead.

On April 24, 1981 they were honored to be chosen to perform on the Capitol Showcase in Albany at the Empire State Performing Arts Center. Bill Knowlton featured them on the *Bluegrass Ramble*, WCNY TV out of Syracuse. And they played over television station WSKG Binghamton, NY.

Displayed in a prominent place on the wall in Mary's home is a plaque the band received in 1982 for their contribution to family oriented bluegrass music. The plaque, from the American Music Conference titled 'Amateur Music Family of the Year' is a Northeast Regional Award and is signed by James W. Johnson, President. Mary recalls their biggest and busiest years were 1980-82.

As the children grew older and pursued other interests it became increasingly difficult to schedule public performances. Mary Sr. says their last performance was probably in 1984. Mary Jr is at present pursuing a career as a singer and songwriter. Joel, the eldest, who did not play in the band is now 47, Rick 43, Tim 40, Jeff 36, Jonathan 31, Joshua 29 and Mary 27.

Ron Parsons
(February 15, 1935 – October 22, 1996)

Ron was a professional truck driver. He grew up in a musical family; his grandfather Clayton Miller and his uncle John Miller were both fiddlers. With this background in music he learned to play the guitar and performed in a country band called **The Country Gentlemen** in the 1960s and 1970s. Band members included Ron on electric guitar, Ray Fogel on bass, Larry Setzer on accordion, Andy Tomsic on fiddle and Lonnie Lipyanic on guitar.

After attending a bluegrass festival at Gettysburg in the early 1970s, Ron became interested in bluegrass. He and his wife Verna, friends Louie and Larry Setzer, Andy Tomsic and Ray Fogel decided to form a bluegrass organization. In 1972 they formed the Appalachian Fiddle and Bluegrass Association with Louie Setzer as the president, Andy Tomsic, vice president and Larry Setzer as the financial secretary. Ron Parsons was chairman of the organization. Within a few years the number of members had increased to several hundred. Ron's son Craig recalled that at one time there were over two thousand members in the organization.

As chairman of the organization, Ron was instrumental in putting on the first festivals at Cline's Grove in Bath, PA. He was also a factor in the organization's decision in 1979 or 1980 to purchase Mountain View Park in Windgap, where there have been annual festivals for the past 20 years. The organization originally held its monthly meetings at the Blueberry Farm Show in Bangor, PA but for the past ten years have met at Edelman's Rod and Gun Club in Belfast.

Ron was well known for his clear piercing voice and the duets he sang with son Craig in the band **The Blue Ridge Mountain Boys**. The early band members included Ron, Craig and Brad Miller playing guitar, Duane Ormsby on dobro, Gary Harper on banjo and Ron Penska on bass. Ron is particularly remembered for his show stopping rendition of his signature song "When The Grass Grows Over Me." In remembrance of his father, Craig always sings that song when the band performs.

Rudy Perkins
(May 18, 1924 – February 18, 1999)

Rudy was born in Virginia and grew up as a younger member of a large family. The family lived in a poor rural hill section and during his early years there was no electricity to power a radio. Thus the only country music heard in the home was performed by family members on stringed instruments. Rudy and an older brother both learned to play the guitar at an early age.

When he was eight years old Rudy collected toke roots and other herbs to sell to the local store to earn twenty-five cents, the price needed for admittance to the **Carter Family** presentation at the local school. Rudy was enthralled by the music and made up his mind that he wanted to learn how to play in their style. When he was eleven he contracted polio and from the time of his recovery until his death he was confined to a wheelchair.

Rudy was about thirteen when the TVA brought electricity to the area and into his home. When the family got their first radio he listened to Bill Monroe playing the mandolin, an instrument he'd never heard of. He remembers hearing them do the gospel song "What Would You Give In Exchange For Your Soul." When the family moved to Pennsylvania he was able to attend a school for the handicapped. He then went on to complete his education at a business college.

In the 1930s Rudy learned to play the mandolin and began to write songs. At that time he was performing and singing one of his songs at Edgemont Park in Allentown, PA. Stoney Cooper and Wilma Lee heard the song and asked him if perhaps they could use it on their next recording. Rudy agreed and thus began a lifelong friendship and business venture with them. From 1955 to

1975 he traveled throughout Pennsylvania with them whenever they were in the area. During his time with Wilma Lee and Stoney Cooper about twenty-five of his songs were recorded, including one of Rudy's most successful, "Row Number 2, Seat Number 3". Rudy was also well acquainted with Alex and Olla Belle Campbell, entertainers, songwriters, recording artists and promoters of Sunset Park in West Grove, PA.

In the past few years Rudy had organized a band called **Rural Delivery** with Bob Parsons on guitar, Lucrezia Woodruff on guitar and singing vocals, Andrew Parsons on bass and Rudy on mandolin. In 1997 regular band members, Rudy, Bob and Lucrezia, recorded a tape titled *Rural Delivery*. The tape was a collection of Rudy's compositions including, "Bring It All Home," "Collection of Broken Hearts," "What Would I Be (Without Your Love)," "Cat Song," "Cried," "Fullness of Time," "Pickers Lament," "Old Wedding Pictures," "Gettin' By," "Walk Slowly" and "Mountain Song." This recording session included guest performers Elmer Hoover on dobro and 5-string, Steve Jacobi on fiddle, Matthew Holgate on bass and David Admantis on guitar. At the time of his death Rudy was under contract with the Rose-Acuff recording company.

To Rudy, the rhythm of the feet, whether toe tapping, dancing, or clogging defined bluegrass music. It also included banjo, acoustic instruments, a quick beat and a blues element.

John Rossbach
(b. April 18, 1954)

John was born in West Virginia and received his college education in Ohio. He then returned to West Virginia before moving to Syracuse, NY in 1984. John says he became interested in bluegrass music when as a three-year-old he heard his father's 78 rpm recording of Bill Monroe's

John Rossbach

"Molly and Tenbrooks." He now makes his living pursuing bluegrass music, his lifetime interest. A former writer for *Bluegrass Unlimited* magazine, John also teaches a course called 'The History of Bluegrass and Old Time Music.' In addition, he is a guitar instructor at the Augusta Heritage Arts Center in West Virginia.

John has played in many bands including **Bristol Mountain Bluegrass, Mac Benford and the Woodshed All-Stars**. His current band, **Chestnut Grove**, includes John on mandolin, Karl Lauber on banjo, Dave Kiphuth on guitar and banjo and Doug Henrie on bass. Karl is a former member of Joe Val's band. Dave has played in bands for both Walt Michaels and Frank Wakefield. Doug played in a family band with his brothers and took first place at the 1976 Galax Old Time Band competition. Perry Cleaveland, who has his own band, sometimes sits in as a guest mandolin player

His bluegrass accomplishments include assignment as IBMA'S Regional Representatives Program Director for four years. He has won four Syracuse Area Music Awards and has been nominated in two categories for 1999. He was the recipient of seven Meet the Composer awards. He has also made appearances on CBS, PBS, BBC and the Canadian Broadcasting System. He appeared with David Holt on Nashville Network's *Fire On The Mountain* a few years ago in a program that was seen coast to coast.

Working both as a single and with his band, John has appeared at over fifty venues in New York State and Pennsylvania including Ashokan Dance Camp, Champlain Valley Folk Festival, the Finger Lakes Grass Roots Festival, the Philadelphia Folk Festival, the Thousand Islands Festival and Winterhawk. John is featured on tapes, CDs and records with Bill Keith, Charles Sawtelle, the Burns Sisters, Don Stover, Ken Perlman, **The Woodshed All-Stars**, Tad Marks and Jolie Christine Rickman.

John says that explaining bluegrass music would take several hours, but a short definition is the 1946 combination of Bill Monroe, Lester Flatt and Earl Scruggs.

Gil Siegers

(b. August 16, 1938)

Gil was born in Brooklyn, NY and lived for a time in Washington State. He later moved to the Endicott, NY area and worked for IBM. He is currently residing in Colorado. When Gil was eight his father bought him an inexpensive five-string banjo. After playing it infrequently Gil put it away until 1974 when he became serious about learning to play it. In 1976 he was living in Washington State and there joined the Washington State Old Time Fiddlers. They met and played at the Curley Creek Dance Hall in Curley Creek, Washington. In 1976 or 1977 Gil entered his first banjo picking contest in Centralia, Washington, playing "Cumberland Mountain Bear Chase" and either "Wildwood Flower" or "Cripple Creek." He did not win.

In 1979 while working for IBM in Endicott, Gil wrote a curriculum for teaching five-string banjo and submitted it to the local BOCES. The program was accepted and from 1979 to about 1984 he taught eleven or twelve banjo courses, mostly for beginners with a few intermediate classes at the Union-Endicott High School. Some of the pupils he remembered included Cathy Pratt Loveland, Bob Hazen, Gale Peabody, Gene Clayton, Jim Pritchard, Randy Cornwell, Leo Strong, Harry Hartz, Ken Oakley and Danny White. For the fall 1980 course Gil persuaded three musicians, Gene Phillips on guitar, Larry Downey on fiddle and Bob Lindsey on banjo, to perform bluegrass music for the class. Gil's son Bobby, a contest banjo player, helped out in the class as a co-instructor.

After an unsuccessful attempt to buy the Ome Banjo Company in 1998, Gil has worked part time for the company as a field representative. He terminated his work with IBM in 1993 and moved to Colorado where he now resides permanently. Gil fondly recalls the picking sessions at the Barn in Gulf Summit. As a train buff he enjoyed the sound of the passing locomotives.

Irene Thurston
(August 26, 192 – March 10, 1992)

Irene was a latecomer to bluegrass music. Until she was 52 she lived in Groton with her husband and raised a family while working at different times for Smith Corona, Groton Senior Citizens Nursing Home, Childrens' Services and as a home health aide. After her husband died in 1977, Irene accompanied her son Wayne to a CNYBA meeting in Cato, New York where she first became interested in bluegrass, especially clogging to the music. From that point on she was hooked. She began to attend local bluegrass festivals and soon joined a number of bluegrass organizations, taking an active part as a member. As she traveled to festivals further from home and became more knowledgeable, Irene began to write articles for a number of bluegrass newsletters including CNYBA and the Del-Se-Nango Country Music Courier.

Irene soon found that the area in front of the stages where bluegrass performances were given was often unsuitable for clogging so she made a small hinged platform that she could put on the ground for dancing. She was welcomed at festivals by the bluegrass promoters and the audiences began to expect to see her clogging whenever she attended a performance. Within a year or two she became known up and down the East Coast from Maine to Florida as the 'Clogging Grandma.' She became a familiar sight clogging on her board at a bluegrass or cajun festival wearing her trademark 'Clogging Grandma' tee shirt.

Irene met her good friend and traveling companion Bill Szabo in 1982. Bill is a retired school attendance officer from Long Island. From 1982 until the time of her death Irene and Bill traveled extensively throughout the United States sightseeing and attending festivals. One year they traveled from Escahog, Maine to California, to Kissimmee, Florida and then to Kingston and Gananoque, Canada, taking in thirty-five festivals. Over the years Irene entered many clogging contests and won her share of them.

Irene Thurston and Bill Szabo

Whenever a local newspaper featured an article about a bluegrass festival being held in the area, the accompanying picture would often show either Irene or Irene and Bill on the clogging board.

Jeff Wisor
(b. November 16, 1940)

Jeff lives in the Corning, NY area. He became interested in music at age fifteen, playing tenor banjo in a square dance band. Al Schutt was the leader of a local band called **The Green Mountain Boys** and his band fronted for Reno and Smiley in 1956. Jeff attended the show and took an immediate interest in bluegrass.

At about that time Jeff had an opportunity to pick with Bucky Walters at the home of Kit Kithcart. Kit took time to show Jeff some licks on the 5-string banjo. In 1962 Jeff took some banjo lessons from Joel Wattstein, a banjo teacher from Long Island.

Jeff played in the area-based band **Mississippi Gamblers** with leader Jim Wallace for two years in the mid 1960s. In 1964 he and wife Marlene joined with Bucky Walters to form the **Voices of Bluegrass**. This band played at the Rock B Tavern in Binghamton, NY. They also traveled to Canada, Alaska and Newfoundland. The band broke up in 1967. In 1968 Jeff moved to Pennsylvania where he played electric guitar in a country band. In 1970 he won the fiddler's championship at Darien Lake, a cash award and a trophy. In the late 1960s he also played fiddle in a Toronto, Canada band called **Home Brew** led by Carol Webb.

Jeff moved to Washington, D.C. in 1972 and there won the Smithsonian Fiddle Contest. For a short time he played in the **Liz Meyer and Friends** band. With Jeff on fiddle and Danny Gatton on guitar, the band played both country and bluegrass music. In 1973 Jeff joined the band **IInd Generation** with Eddie Adcock on banjo, Gene

Johnson on mandolin, Wendy Thatcher on guitar, Jimmy Gadreau on mandolin and John Castle on bass. While with Eddie, Jeff fiddled for three albums produced by Rebel.

After leaving the Adcock group Jeff played for **Night Sun** with Gene Johnson on mandolin, Dick Smith on banjo, John Castle on bass, Scott McElhaney on guitar and Jeff on fiddle. They played at one of the first bluegrass festivals in Corinth NY. The group also won the 'Most Promising Vocal Group' award at the 1976 Muleskinner News Award Show, beating out **Boone Creek** led by Ricky Scaggs.

In 1978 Jeff moved to Nashville and played fiddle for Jeanne Shepard and Donna Fargo. In 1979 he was back in D.C. where he played with David Bromberg from 1980 to 1993. In 1989 Jeff won the New York State Fiddling Championship. In 1990 he recorded "Sideman Serenade" with Bromberg who retired in 1993. Returning to Nashville in 1994 he become part of a group consisting of Eddie and Martha Adcock and Eddie Sykes for a year.

Along with other accomplishments Jeff traveled to Russia with the **Corning Grass Works.** He also toured in Europe with Sharon Cort, Ernie Sykes, Butch Baldassari and Bill Keith. From 1995 to the present he has played with **Burnt Toast**, a Pennsylvania-based band.

Bluegrass Humor

Virtually no organization, party or gathering of friends is without its lighter moments and bluegrass is certainly no exception. Besides hearing the music they like played live by favorite performers, people also enjoy bluegrass festivals for the fun of humorous episodes that occur there as well as hearing about them later. There are few festivals where high jinx and shenanigans are not present. Some events have been carefully orchestrated, others are completely spontaneous. Festival goers have witnessed and or participated in mock weddings, with a full panoply of attendants and guests and ceremonies. Elaborate candlelight dinners with silver, crystal and fine wine are enjoyed by elegantly attired hosts and their guests. Episodes involving cross dressing are recurrent. Sight gags are prevalent. Practical jokes are commonplace. Good-natured heckling of the bands performing on stage is not uncommon and many times the bands heckle the crowds. Following is a selection of anecdotes that reflect the happy camaraderie experienced at a bluegrass festival.

Hawaiian Bluegrass

At a Laing Family Festival at Bainbridge one year Bill Harrell and fellow band members appeared on stage wearing flamboyant colorful Hawaiian shirts. Imagine the crowd's delight when Bill's son Mitch showed up on stage wearing a lei and a grass hula skirt.

Anything Goes Band

Some bands invite a great many people to play on stage with them. Someone at Wrench Wranch suggested a set with very nontraditional instruments. The cacophony of multiple stick thumpers, rock bangers, pan clangers, kazoo tooters and even a trombone blower was truly unforgettable.

No smoking

About ten years ago, a wanna-be stage performer showed up at the barn in Gulf Summit and announced that he'd like to play on stage at one of the Penny festivals. He was told that all he had to do was join Penny and show up at the Ransom Park festival with his guitar.

While he was at the barn, he noticed a sign which said 'Penny Members - No Smoking!' Thinking that the sign meant that when an individual joined Penny he had to quit smoking, he reluctantly agreed to give up cigarettes. Some time later the new Penny member showed up at Ransom Park, with his guitar and ready to play. He was told that he would have to audition before he could play on stage, and even then he might not be selected. As he looked around the area he noticed several people smoking. Quickly he asked, "Are they Penny members?" When told they were he asked "Can Penny members smoke here?" When told they could, he quickly lit up.

Sweet Things Production Company

Carol Ripic's musical ambition was to play in an all-female bluegrass band. She had a taste of that experience at the 1988 Penny Memorial Festival when she filled in on bass for Betty Conklin in a group with Barbara LaPointe and Debbie Clark on banjo and Billie Karcher on guitar. The dream, however, was not realized until midwinter 1989 when Carol gave some thought to starting her own all-girl band. However, since female bluegrass players were the exception, she asked three male friends, John Evanick, Clint Lainhart and Ken Oakley, if they would consider dressing as women to play in an all-girl band. They agreed and Sweet Things was born.

Ken decided that since the group was going to play at the upcoming Wrench Wranch festival, then Ted Wrench ought to at least be aware of it. After letting Ted know what to expect, Ken asked Ted to join them on stage. With encouragement from his wife Brenda, Ted agreed.

At the 1989 Memorial Day Festival the unsuspecting crowd was astounded to see Clint, Ken and John appear on the stage in drag accompanied by Carol appropriately dressed in female garb. With Clint on banjo, John playing dobro, Ken picking the guitar and Carol on the bass the crowd was treated to several lively bluegrass selections. But the best was yet to come. When 'Theodora' Wrench was introduced the unbelieving fans ran for videos and cameras to record his/her splendor in a blue, flowered dress, wig, earrings and matching bonnet. Ted lived up to everyone's expectations with his 'heart-wrenching wrendition' of "Don't Say Goodbye If You Love Me." More was to come.

A year or two later, one of the Sweet Things got the idea that the bluegrass music scene needed grass with class. So the 1992 Memorial Day Weekend Festival crowd was treated to a string ensemble called String Things with Gil Loveland on violin, Cathy Loveland on viola, Ken Oakley on cello and Carol Ripic on bowed bass. The women wore white blouses with black flowing skirts and the men, what else, tux jackets and bow ties. Peter Plain as conductor stole the show as he performed in front of the stage on a little podium with his classically held baton. Under Peter's leadership the band played the classic, "Boilen Dem Cabbages Downen," "Ragtime Antoinette," with its classy pizzicato and the ever popular "Supplication Mai'den." Following those three numbers, the entrance of Theodore Von Wrench wearing his tiny derby, straight from the McDonough Opera House brought the house down. There wasn't a dry eye in the place as he fiddled "Cinders a la Passione," sometimes known as "Ashes of Love." After the show a keen-eyed Ken Hockstetler mentioned to Oakley that the group would have done better to cut the tux jackets out of old raincoats. Ken replied, "Bingo."

String Things
L to R: Gil Loveland, Carol Ripic, Ken Oakley, Cathy Loveland

String Things was followed by the performance of Little Things at the Wrench Wranch Festival that fall. Gale Peabody lowered the mikes to two or three feet for midget-sized performers. Emcee Bill Knowlton introduced the band as Clint Lainhart, Ken Oakley, Carol Ripic and Julie Maxwell trouped out on stage. Wearing shoes taped to their knees, Clint played a half sized guitar, Ken, a small banjolin. Carol's bass was actually a cello and Julie made her stage debut playing a mini-tambourine. All were dressed in 'little people' clothes with short pants or skirts. After a few 'short' numbers the featured performer was ushered on stage. Again the audience was stunned when Ted Wrench strode on stage, on his knees, wearing a 'little people' coverall. He then proceeded to give a short 'wrendition' of "Two Little Boys." At this point people in the audience were beginning to realize that when Sweet Things performed, they should expect to see a guest appearance by Ted.

The next Sweet Things production took place at the 1993 Memorial Day Weekend Festival. Sing Sing Things presented more of a story than the previous presentations. After Brenda Wrench, the hanging judge, introduced the prisoners, their crimes and sentences, Clint Lainhart, Carol Ripic, Ken Oakley and Julie Maxwell appeared on stage wearing prison stripes and dragging a ball and chain. Billie Karcher wore a blue jump-suit as the prison 'trusty.' After doing a few prison songs like "Shackles and Chains" and "Take This Hammer," Julie escaped. After weaving through the crowd, chased by Billie, Julie disappeared behind the kitchen. Soon Billie appeared alone, walked to the stage and complained over the mike, "She got away." Just about then Ted Wrench, in a state trooper's uniform, appeared with Julie in tow. "How did you catch her when I could not?" asked Billie. Officer Ted then launched into his song, "I Traced Her Little Footprints in The Dirt."

The last appearance of Sweet Things took place at the 1993 Wrench Wranch Festival in the fall. This time the group did a spoof on the *Beverly Hillbillies*. Brenda Wrench as Mrs. Drysdale introduced the group that included Ken Oakley as Jed, Carol Ripic as Ellie May, Clint Lainhart as Granny and Julie Maxwell as Cousin Pearl. The group featured new lyrics for the show's standard songs, jokes and puns. Mrs. Drysdale introduced Flatt and Scruggs aptly portrayed by Shawn Batho and Tom Benson. When they finished "Flint Hill Special," Mrs. Drysdale led Jethro, that is Ted Wrench, on stage dragging him by the ear.

When Jed asked Jethro to play the "Orange Blossom Special" the rehearsed refusal became a taped version played over the sound system. With that presentation, Sweet Things Production Company called it a day.

All The Good Names

In 1989 Jim Hannigan hosted a bluegrass festival at DiLeos in Mill City, PA. It was there that the author met an interesting individual in bib overalls who was indeed a local farmer. The fact that he had a New England accent only lends a bit more color to the story. When asked his name he drawled with what seemed to be distinct distaste, "My name is Orren." When asked what was wrong with his name he replied, "I don't like it." He continued with this explanation. "My father was a farmer. He had cows, horses, chickens, dogs and cats. And he had names for all of them." Here he paused to let that last fact set in. "By the time I was bawn, all the good names were gawn."

Barney Stories

Among the area's many fine guitars pickers, the best would have to include Doug Trotter, Tim Walbridge, Marc Chevalier and Barney French. Of these four, Barney could do things on a guitar which almost defy description, like lightning fast breaks, clear Norman Blake licks, outstanding backup and 'home-made' chords. He's been seen to bar a fret with his first finger and reach six frets with his pinkie to get an unusual sound. In addition to his playing ability Barney has a very sharp wit and unique way with words.

Barney and the Cat

At the 1988 Ransom Park Festival, Barney was a member of a late-night picking session. When the party broke up all went to their respective campers to catch a little sleep. Except for Barney. Not having a camper to go to and not wanting to drive home, Barney fell asleep in a convenient lawn chair. When morning arrived Barney was sound asleep with a small cat curled up in the hollow of his neck. When he awoke, Barney swore that the cat had stolen his brain.

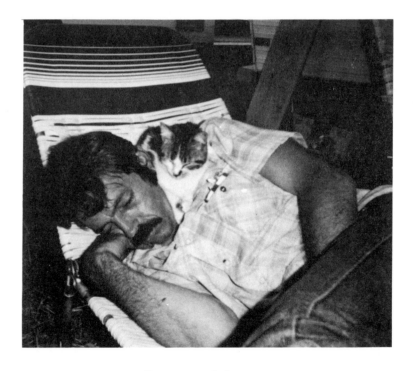

Barney and the Cat

The Philosopher

At about this time period and at the same Ransom Park Festival, Barney and Doug Lesch were sharing their viewpoints on life and Doug had just made an insightful remark. Not to be outdone, Barney replied, "Well, I have noticed that just about every time thirty days pass, a month goes by."

Doug, not being able to top that one, decided to change the subject. "Are you married?" he asked Barney. Barney said, "Well I was married once quite a few years ago. One day I took my wife to the beauty parlor and she asked me to pick her up in about an hour. On my way home I got to wondering just what I was doing, being married, and when I got home I packed some things, got my guitar and left. Never went back." Here Barney paused, musing, "God, she must be beautiful by now!"

The Portajohn

This anecdote was related by Dale Maxwell. When Barney went to visit the facilities at Ransom Park one evening, his friends waited until the door closed and then backed a pickup truck firmly against the door. When Barney tried to exit he found his way was blocked. The perpetrators expected the worst kind of explosion from Barney after taunting him with the inimitable sound of liquid refreshment tops popping. Just then Barney was heard to say, "Listen up boys," followed by his own popping top sound. At that, chagrined, the group silently pushed the truck away, freeing the door. Barney, supplied with his own six-pack and in no hurry, did not realize he was now free and stayed right there until someone opened the door.

Bedding Down For The Night

The Booze Brothers were performing at Wrench Wranch for the Penny Memorial Day Weekend Fest in the late 1980s. They had all stayed up late doing some parking lot picking. One early riser saw Gary Harper sitting on a stool drinking his first coffee of the day. This individual remarked that Gary's eyes looked pretty bad. "You should see them from my side," he replied. Then the early riser asked Gary where Barney might be. With that Gary ambled over to a nearby pickup truck, got down gingerly on his knees and searched the ground under the truck. "I don't know," he said. "His bed hasn't been slept in."

Trip to Old Mill Village

This anecdote was related second or third hand. One day Barney French, Charlie Kutney and Peter Plain, bluegrassers all, were traveling to Old Mill Village in New Milford, PA for the Fall music contest when the muffler fell off the car. They were about to leave the the muffler where it lay when one of the trio opined that the Pennsylvania State Police were ruthless when finding an out-of-state car with no muffler. So they fastened the broken muffler to the back fender and proceeded on their way.

Festival Boredom

If a male bluegrass stage performer's wife doesn't play an instrument and isn't exactly crazy about the camping out bit, it's possible for her to get a little bored with the long weekend stretching ahead. Janelle Clayton, Marilyn Lubeck and a few other young ladies found a momentary respite at Dale Maxwell's Schuyler, NY Festival in 1986. This group of six or seven ladies took their lawn chairs to the area where an older man was emptying the portajohns. They set their chairs in a semi-circle about fifty feet away and cheered and clapped when the ministrations were completed. When the action moved to another station, the women moved also. When the performance was over, they each dutifully took their programs up to the man for his autograph.

The Uninvited Guest

At a summer festival about fifteen years ago Ted Wrench picked and partied long and hard one night. The way back to his camper was dark and he was tired and a bit tipsy. As he was negotiating his way toward his camper and some well-deserved sleep he somehow found that a small pup tent had sprung up in his path.

Blundering forward, he became tangled in the guy ropes and fell into the middle of the tent arousing the two people sleeping inside. Mumbling a few words of apology, Ted continued on his way, leaving the two startled campers to deal with a pile of canvas, poles and rope.

Unnecessary retake

This anecdote was related by Bill Knowlton. The 52 half-hour segments of the *Bluegrass Ramble* program presented over television station WCNY, Syracuse were taped live. In all those shows few retakes were necessary. A memorable one involved a performance by the Spirits of Bluegrass. The Spirits had a fiddle player and vocalist named Dave Lightcap who did a number where he breaks into tears at the end of each chorus of the song as part of the act. One of the TV directors, not knowing this, stopped shooting in the middle of the song and went out on the stage to help poor Dave. A retake was in order.

The Two Piece Bass

This anecdote was related by Bucky Walters. Frank Wakefield, now living in the Albany, NY area, is a virtuoso mandolin player. He's originated outlandish licks, written high speed instrumentals and played in any number of big name bands. He's also known as one who sometimes marches to a different drummer. At the time of this incident Frank was playing, along with George Shuffler, in Jimmy Martin's band. For transportation Jimmy and the band were touring in a big red Cadillac. Following a performance Jimmy asked Frank to stow the bass in the Caddy. After trying unsuccessfully to fit the recalcitrant instrument into the trunk of the car, he hit upon a pragmatic solution. When the band arrived at the next playing engagement, Jimmy was astonished to find that the top of the bass had been sawed off just above the pegs.

Joe Bonifanti, Frank Wakefield, Whitey Shultz

Sharing a Dressing Room

This anecdote was related by Chris Panfil. In the 1970s Creek Bend, a very young high energy and irreverent bluegrass band from Buffalo, NY believed that the only way to get good was to play often on stage. They felt this so strongly that they took a regular weekly booking just across the border in Ft. Erie, Ontario. At the King Edward Hotel they alternated half-hour sets with a live exotic dancer. "We were very excited about sharing dressing rooms," Chris said.

Are We There Yet?

A bluegrasser was going to Gettysburg for a festival one weekend in the 1980s. When he stopped at a gas station another camper pulled up and the driver asked if he were going to Gettysburg. When he said that he was, the other man asked for directions. "I'm going there now. Why don't you follow me?" he replied and off they went. About an hour later the lead camper's driver realized that he'd missed a turnoff and that he'd have to turn around and go back. However he didn't want to answer any questions from the man following. "I know what I'll do," he thought, "I'll lose him." With that he accelerated. But the second camper kept right up. About that time there appeared a right turnoff just over a rise in the road. The lead camper turned off the dirt road and drove furiously for about a mile. Looking back through the rising dust he could see that the man was still with them. Turning down a second dirt turnoff, he felt he could surely lose the camper following. After about a hundred yards he came to a timber across the road. It was a dead end. Just then the man who'd been following them drove up in his camper. He got out and said, "Are we there yet?"

Purist Instrument

The bluegrass purists will tell us that there are only five bluegrass instruments, maybe six if you allow the dobro. The other five are fiddle, five-string banjo, guitar, bass and mandolin. Imagine the consternation of these purists when they caught a glimpse of the 'toilet-tone'. The neck is a copy of the Gibson Mastertone neck, although it has been shortened to permit open C tuning. The rim came from an old five-string banjo, and the flange is, you guessed it, a old toilet seat. To make the instrument fully complete, a 1939 Ford hubcap is the resonator. As far as is known, the 'toilet-tone' is a one-of-a-kind instrument.

Toilet Tone Banjo

Bluegrass Barnyard

This anecdote was related by Gene Clayton. While setting up one of the early Ransom Park Festivals Gene's wife received a phone call asking if it would be ok to bring a goat to the festival. The caller said that they wanted to attend the festival but that the goat had to be milked regularly so they couldn't leave it at home. Janelle said she thought it would be all right and so a goat was tethered in the parking lot throughout the festival.

The Banjo lesson

Understand that the author is not a terrific banjo player. However, knowing just enough to be dangerous, he entered a banjo contest at the Old Mill Village in Montrose, PA in August 1991. It just so happened that this particular year, for some reason or another, the author won. Probably the other contestants, Carl Kithcart, Jim Benson and Bob Lindsey, were all better banjo players. However, they were gracious in their acceptance of 2nd, 3rd and 4th places.

However the foolish winner could not leave it at that. No, he waited until his band performed on stage at Wrench Wranch the very next month, where he had the temerity to suggest to Jim Benson and Carl Kithcart, who were in the crowd that day, that he would give them free banjo lessons for the asking. Later that day when in the midst of performing the band's second set, a dozen or so banjo players led by Carl Kithcart showed up at the corner of the stage. They requested that the 'champion' banjo player show them how to play "Redwing" right then. How the author got through the number he'll never know. And it was a good thing that there was no one there with a tape recorder. Carl followed the tried and true maxim of a victim. Don't get mad, get even. Score Carl - 1, Ken - 0.

Snip City Mayor

Pat Parsnow isn't content to go to a bluegrass festival, set up camp and generally relax. He likes to inaugurate a happening. One year at Wrench Wranch he decided to run for mayor of Snip City, his borough. Ballots were distributed and Pat won by a landslide. This reoccurred the following year when he again won the election. However, the third year Paps Grant got wind of the election and decided to run against the incumbent. Paps had flyers printed and campaigned at various campsites, promising all sort of things like excellent weekend weather, free food and showers. To prevent any voting fraud, the ballot box was stationed in the pavilion and a guard posted. Paps did win the election but not without a hearty fight from Pat.

More Monitor, Please

In 1991 Jim Hannigan hosted a bluegrass festival at Fleetville, PA. Jim asked the band about to go on stage if his daughter Jamie, then a preschooler, could do a number called "Little Raindrop". The band members thought she'd just come up on stage and start right in with her song. Imagine their surprise when she walked up to the mike which the sound man had lowered for her and said in a very clear voice, "Check one, check two, a little more monitor please."

Bluegrass Impersonators

This anecdote was related by Bill Laing. Bill was working as a car salesman in the late 1970s. He, brother Gil and their wives, Doreen and Ann, drove a big red Cadillac to the Afton Fair to the see the Osborne Brothers perform. When they got to the gate, Bill told the ticket taker that he was Sonny Osborne and that Gil in the back seat was Bobby. The gatekeeper was impressed to be meeting such stars and allowed them to pass through, telling them where to park in the performer's area. Bill parked the car in the regular customer's area and then went to the gate to pay the group's admission fees. A few years later when Sonny and Bobby were performing at the Laing Family Festival, Bill told them this story. Sonny later told the same story to Ralph Embry on Embry's national television show over TNN.

The Largest Band

Most prominent bands find a suitable name and stick with it. Ted Wrench has successfully defied that concept by changing the name of his band about as often as a society matron changes hair color. Over the past fifteen years names for Ted's group have included The Happy Hollow Boys, Happy Hollow Folks, Wrench's Wramblings, Wrench's Wranglers, Wrench's Wramblers, Wrench's Warblers, Ted and The Truckers, Ted and The Boys and Wrench's Prime Timers. At the present time the group seems to have gotten stuck on Wrench's Wranglers. At least that's the name listed on the most recent band lineup announcement.

Not only has the band name changed frequently, so has its composition. Over the years the list of players reads like a telephone directory. Memory limits the mention of all members, but a few of the regulars have included Matt Arnold, Shaun Batho, Jim Benson, Chris Brown, Lou Brown, Chris Bubney, Jim and Arlene Callan, Dave Cavage, Gene Clayton, Scott Corbett, Steve Di-Rancho, Bob Daugherty, Al Eddy, Bud Fish, Joe Ganna, Jim Hannigan, Gary Harper, Ken Hockstetler, Dennis Johnson, Billie Karcher, Carl Kithcart, Clint Lainhart, Doug Lesch, Daryl Lesch, John Lubeck, Duane Ormsby,

Pat Parsnow, Terry Patrick, Gale Peabody, Ron Penska, Tom Quigley, John Rumberg, Bob Schneider, Claude Sherwood, Whitey Shultz, Gordie Sutton, Doug Trotter and Lance Trotter, Kevin Whalen, Duke Wilson, Becky Yonts and many others.

Fritzisms

Ray Fritz was well-known for his unique perspective on many things. For example, he would allow that in cases of capital crime there sometimes just might be extenuating circumstances which provoked the perpetrator. For these offenses, Ray would condone leniency. However, for those heinous individuals who blocked his driveway or parked their vehicle illegally, Ray would repeat time and time again, "They orter be hung."

Likewise, Ray had no patience with the lawmakers who allowed authorities to postpone work on a dam project until a home could be found for the endangered snail darter, a small fish found only in the Tennessee River and its tributaries. Many times he was heard to say, "They held up that project for years fiddlin' around with the dang snail darter. Why save it? It was too small for eatin' and too big for bait."

More Bass

One of the truly great practical jokes perpetrated on a band happened at the Wrench Wranch in the mid 1980s. During the evening performance of The Booze Brothers, sound man Gale Peabody gradually lowered the volume on bass player Al Eddy's microphone. Each time Gale lowered the bass mike's volume, a few co-conspirators in the audience yelled, "More bass!"

Meanwhile, a dozen bass players, each carrying a bass, quietly lined on the stage behind the band. When the interlopers began to play, an astonished Al turned around to see what was going on. The band appreciated the joke that had been played on them. The audience loved it and the twelve bass players really enjoyed themselves. Gloria Parsnow took a picture that was printed on tee shirts, some of which are still around.

Bibliography

Berbaum, Ed and Geraldine Mendel Berbaum. "The Jehihle Kirkfuff Story." *The Old Time Hearald Journal.* Spring 1993: 12-17.

Bronner, Simon J. *Old time music makers of New York State.* Syracuse, NY: Syracuse University Press, c1987.

Chapman, Richard. *The Complete guitarist.* New York: Dorling Kindersley, c1993.

Diagram Group. *Musical instruments of the world: an illustrated encyclopedia.* Paddington Press Ltd./The Two Continents Publishing Group, c1976.

Fraizer, Charles. *Cold Mountain.* New York: Atlantic Monthly Press, c1997.

Kinder, Gary. *Ship of gold in the deep blue sea.* New York: Atlantic Monthly Press, c1988.

Kingsbury, Paul, ed. *Encyclopedia of country music.* New York: Oxford University Press, 1998.

Kochman, Marilyn, ed. *The Big book of bluegrass.* New York: Quill/A Frets Book, c1984.

Longworth, Mike. *Martin guitars: a history,* Minisink Hills, PA: Four Maples Press, c1988.

McCloud, Barry and others. *Definitive country: the ultimate encyclopedia of country music and its performers.* New York: Berkley Publishing Group, c1995.

Rosenberg, Neil V. *Bluegrass: a history.* Chicago: University of Illinois Press, c1985.

Scruggs, Earl. *Earl Scruggs and the 5-string banjo*. New York: Peer International Corporation, c1968.

Sherman, Tony. "Country." *American Heritage*: November 1994: 38-57.

Smith, Richard D. *Bluegrass: an informal guide*. Chicago: a capella books, c1995.

Washburn, Jim and Richard Johnson. *Martin Guitars: an illustrated celebration of America's premier guitarmaker*. Emmaus, PA: Rodale Press, c1997.

Wood, Leslie C. *Holt! T'other way!*. Middletown, PA: Leslie C. Wood, 1950.

Wood, Leslie, C. *Rafting on the Delaware*. Middletown, PA: Leslie C. Wood, 1950.

New York State Organizations

Addison - Southern Tier Bluegrass Association
Bennington - Western New York Old Time & BluegrassAssn.
Cato - Central New York Bluegrass Association
Clayton - Thousand Island Bluegrass Association
Corinth - Adirondack Bluegrass League
Coventryville - Pennsylvania New York County &
     Bluegrass Association
Crown Point - Champlain Valley Bluegrass & Old Time
     Music Association
Lindenhurst - Long Island Bluegrass League
New Berlin - Del-Se-Nango
Osceola - New York State Old Time Fiddlers' Association
Poughkeepsie - Hudson Valley Bluegrass Association
Steamburg - Stateline Old Time Country & Bluegrass Assn.
Wilmington - High Peaks Bluegrass League

Northeastern Pennsylvania Organizations

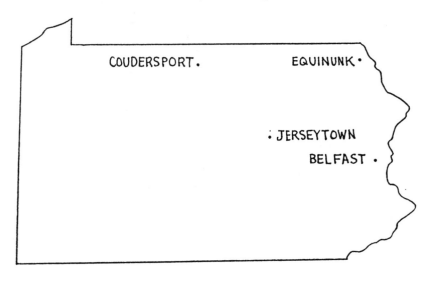

Coudersport - Allegheny Mountain Old Time Music Assn.
Equinunk - Fiddlin' Around
Jerseytown - Country Western Bluegrass Shindig
Belfast - Appalachian Fiddle & Bluegrass Association

Defunct Festival Sites

Festivals are no longer being held at the sites indicated on the maps.

Afton, Bainbridge, Bath, Bridgewater, Catskill, Canisteo, Duanesburg, Elmira, Gardiner, Hannibal,Herkimer, Maine, Marietta Meredian, New Paltz, Otisco Lake, Owego, Oxford, Pulaski, Sandy Creek, Savona, Schroon Lake, Schuyler, Syracuse in New York State.

Dalton, Fleetville, Jerseytown, Lake Winola, Little Meadows, Merryall, Meshoppen, Ransom in Northeastern Pennsylvania.

New York State

DEFUNCT FESTIVALS

SCHROON LAKE

. SANDY CREEK
 .PULASKI
.HANNIBAL
MEREDIAN.   SCHUYLER . .HERKIMER
                          .BRIDGEWATER   .DUANESBURG
MARIETTA .   .SYRACUSE
               .OTISCO LAKE

               OXFORD. .BAINBRIDGE   CATSKILL
BATH . .SAVONA   MAINE. .AFTON
CANISTEO.   .KELLYSTON PK
          ELMIRA . OWEGO
                              NEW .PALTZ
                              .GARDINER

Pennsylvania

                          .LITTLE MEADOWS
MESHOPPEN .   .MERRYALL
               .FLEETVILLE
LAKE WINOLA .   .DALTON
              .RANSOM

          JERSEYTOWN

DEFUNCT FESTIVALS

Current New York State Festivals

Addison - STBA Bluegrass Festival
Ancramdale - Winterhawk
Bainbridge - Opry House
Coventryville - Penny Memorial Day Festival
            - Wrench Wranch Wroundup
Clayton - Thousand Islands Bluegrass Festival
Corinth - Corinth Bluegrass Festival
Ellenville - Hotel Fallsview Festival
Ft. Ann - Country Music and Bluegrass Festival
Galway - ABL Roundup
Gouverneur - St. Lawrence Valley Bluegrass Festival
Greenwich Village - Big Apple Festival
Homer - Bluegrass on the Green
        - Bluegrass Ramble
La Fayette - CNYBA Bluegrass Festival
Lodi - Pickin' in the Pasture

Newark Valley - Newark Valley Bluegrass Festival
Nichols - L & L Campground Bluegrass Festival
Norwich - Family Bluegrass Festival
Old Forge-Fox Family Festival
Shinhopple - Peaceful Valley Bluegrass Festival
Steamburg - Old Time Country & Bluegrass Festival
Watkins Glen - Old Time Fiddlers' Gathering

Current Northeastern Pennsylvania Festivals

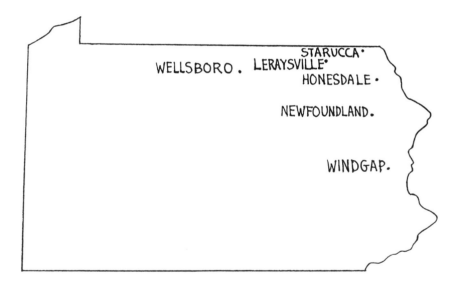

Honesdale - Autumn Leaves Traditional & Dance Festival
LeRaysville - Fire ball Bluegrass Festival
Newfoundland - Blue Smoke and Bluegrass Festival
Starucca - Starucca Bluegrass Festival
Wellsboro - Canyon Country
Windgap - AFBA Bluegrass Festival
        - Windgap Bluegrass Festival

Index

Index

Index

Cornwell, Randy, 56,57,151
Corsair, Arthur, 14
Cort, Sharon, 155
Cortright, Laura, 98,102,103
Cortright, Mike, 103
Corwin, Tammy, 50
Coursey, Joe, 61
Cox, Ronny, 47
Crawford, Dennis, 57
Crawford, Marjorie, 23,24,52,57,79
Crockett, Steve, 82
Cross, Butch, 57
Cross, Lee, 57,80,81,85,136
Crouch, Ray, 52
Crowe, J.D., 52
Crowell, Peg, 61
Crowley, Dick, 63
Cruickshank, Joyce, 52
Cullen, Joyce, 54
Czajowski, Gene, 126

Dadovich, Eddie, 21
Dalhart, Vernon, 29
Daniels, 'Happy' Bill, 14,15
Davey, Jim, 72, 73
Davey, Steve, 72
Davis, Cleo, 35
Davoli, Joe Jr., 111
Day, Bill, 126
Dear, Don, 51
Decker, Al, 57
Delaney, Clayton, 129
Delaney, John, 72,78,79,81,94,98,111
Delaney, Ray, 72,78,79,81,94,98,111
Delmore, Alton, 30
Delmore, Raybon, 30
DeMarco, Tony, 99
Demp, Bob, 124
Dennis, Duane, 60,72
Denny, Dave, 57,102,126
DeNeve, Dick, 50,51
Dibble, Nelson, 61
Dickey, James, 47
Diffendorf, Doris, 129
Diggin, Trevor, 104
Dillard, Doug, 45,47,74
Dillard, Mike, 95,104
Dillard, Rodney, 45,47

Dimick, Lisa, 95,143
Dimick, Randy, 95,143
Dingler, Ben, 17
Dingler, Bob, 17
Dingler, David, 17
Dingler, Denny, 17
Dingler, Don, 17
Dingler, George, 17
Dingler, John, 17
Dingler, William, 16,17
DiRancho, Steve, 75,95,142,171
Dobrosielski, Dick, 130,131
Dopera, John, 8
Dougherty, Bob, 88,171
Downey, Larry, 23,56,102,106,112,
   114,151
Downs, Sandi, 98
Drake, Tom, 62
Duffy, John, 136
Dutra, Dan, 122
Dylan, Bob, 30

Eanes, Jim, 37
Eastman, Charles, 14
Eddy, Al, 89,126,171
Eddy, Carl, 75
Edison, Thomas, 25
Edwards, Dewey, 99
Edwards, George, 99
Ellis, Doug, 95
Elmer, 'Crazy', 67,138,142
Embry, Ralph, 171
Erdman, Bobbe, 93,120
Errigo, Joann, 102,107
Evanick, John, 143,158
Evans, Al, 84,139
Evans, Bruce, 109
Evans, Thelma, 84,139

Fagan, Trudy, 92
Faier, Billy, 40
Fairchild, Raymond, 102
Fargo, Donna, 155
Farrell, Tim, 142
Farren, Charles, 123
Feinberg, Ron, 115
Feinbloom, Steve, 53,54
Ferris, Ed, 136

Index

Index

Index

Index

Index

Index

Index

Index

A Note about the Typeface

The typeface used in this book is Palatino. Designed by Hermann Zapf for the Stempel foundry in 1950, Palatino is one of the most widely used type faces in the world today. The Classical Italian Renaissance elegance of its letters and its Twentieth Century crispness of line make it extremely easy to read in its regular or italics style.